DATE DUE

rder

PRINTED IN U.S.A.

Living with Bipolar Disorder

A Guide for Individuals and Families

Updated Edition

Michael W. Otto, Ph.D.
Noreen A. Reilly-Harrington, Ph.D.
Robert O. Knauz, Ph.D.
Aude Henin, Ph.D.
Jane N. Kogan, Ph.D.
Gary S. Sachs, M.D.

OXFORD
UNIVERSITY PRESS

OXFORD
UNIVERSITY PRESS

Oxford University Press, Inc., publishes works that further
Oxford University's objective of excellence
in research, scholarship, and education.

Oxford   New York

Auckland   Cape Town   Dar es Salaam   Hong Kong   Karachi
Kuala Lumpur   Madrid   Melbourne   Mexico City   Nairobi
New Delhi   Shanghai   Taipei   Toronto

With offices in

Argentina   Austria   Brazil   Chile   Czech Republic   France   Greece
Guatemala   Hungary   Italy   Japan   Poland   Portugal   Singapore
South Korea   Switzerland   Thailand   Turkey   Ukraine   Vietnam

Published by Oxford University Press, Inc.
198 Madison Avenue, New York, New York 10016
www.oup.com

Oxford is a registered trademark of Oxford University Press

Library of Congress Cataloging-in-Publication Data

Living with bipolar disorder: a guide for individuals and families/
Michael W. Otto . . . [et al.].
    p. cm.
    ISBN 978-0-19-978202-4
    1. Manic-depressive illness—Popular works. I. Otto, Michael W.
    RC516.L58 2011
    616.89'5—dc22

                                                    2010031148

3 5 7 9 8 6 4

Printed in the United States of America
on acid-free paper

Dedications

MWO: For my son, Jackson, a source of unending joy

NR-H: With all my love for my husband, Joe, and our three beautiful sons, Joseph, Kevin, & Owen

ROK: To my son, Alex who reminds me to dream big every day

AH: ⬚⬚⬚ husband Sean and son Maxim, with all my love

⬚⬚⬚ ightest lights in my life, Henry and Nora, with love

⬚⬚⬚ e, your grace, support, and humor are the enduring

Contents

Acknowledgments   *ix*

Part 1
Understanding Bipolar Disorder and Its Treatment

1 Introduction   3
2 Description of Bipolar Disorder   5
3 Medication Names and Common Dosages   17
4 Getting in the Habit of Taking Medications   27
5 Psychotherapy for Bipolar Disorder   33
6 Bipolar Disorder in Adolescents and Children   39

Part II
Managing Your Disorder

7 Stress and Schedule Management   57
8 Attention to Thinking Biases   75
9 Relationships and Communication Skills   85
10 Managing Irritability and Anger   93
11 Focusing on Life Goals   101
12 Mood Charting   109
13 Creating a Treatment Contract   115
14 Improving Wellbeing   125

Index   129

Acknowledgments

This book was designed for individuals with bipolar disorder, their families, and clinicians who help their patients manage the disorder. It provides useful information and strategies that everyone affected by this disorder should have. The interventions included in this book were shaped by our collaborations with a number of teams of clinicians and clinical researchers as well as by the patients with whom we have worked. In particular, we would like to thank and acknowledge the input of our colleagues in the very large, NIMH-funded, Systematic Treatment Enhancement Program for Bipolar Disorder (STEP-BD). Our perspectives on treatment were further influenced by independent studies led by Ellen Frank, Dominic Lam, David Miklowitz, and Jan Scott. Likewise, we learned the value of attending to the promotion of wellbeing from research by Giovanni Fava. Useful comments on early versions of this book were provided by a variety of members of the STEP-BD program, including valued feedback from David Miklowitz and Ellen Frank. We thank all of these individuals for expanding what is known about the nature and treatment of bipolar disorder.

Part 1

Understanding Bipolar Disorder and Its Treatment

1

Introduction

This book provides you with a wealth of information on the nature and treatment of bipolar disorder as well as strategies designed to reduce the likelihood of future episodes of depression or mania. In addition to written information, separate Self-Guided Care boxes are used to provide you with opportunities to rehearse self-care activities. These are designed to help you be an active force in coping with your disorder and enhancing your enjoyment of life. Also, all of the strategies in this book are designed for use in conjunction with your treatment team—the doctors, therapists, family members, and others you select as your support system. Near the end of this book, you will be asked to create a treatment contract to inform your treatment team and your support network how to recognize possible periods of illness and the strategies you want them to use to take good care of you.

To get the most benefit from this book, take your time reading and, if you wish, jump from chapter to chapter to focus on those sections most relevant to you at any given time. We would, however, like you to devote time to every chapter of the book to get the most of the strategies and information provided to enhance your control of bipolar disorder. In addition, use the information provided to be a better consumer of the treatments available to you and a better contributor to the treatment decision-making process.

One of the first suggestions for you as an active collaborator in your treatment is to begin thinking about building your support network. Namely, with whom do you want to share this book? The goal is to make your support team even more valuable to you by giving them information about bipolar disorder and a common vocabulary for discussing treatment. Having the family members and friends that you choose read the book is one way to make them more valuable collaborators in your care. Take some time to think about whom you would like to be a part of your support network, and begin to fill out the first Self-Guided Care box.

Self-Guided Care: Selecting Members of Your Support Group

Who might you select because they are supportive individuals?

_____

_____

_____

Who might you select because they have an important impact on your life?

_____

_____

_____

Who might you select in order to improve their understanding of bipolar disorder and how to be helpful to you?

_____

_____

_____

2

Description of Bipolar Disorder

Bipolar disorder, also known as manic depression, is a common psychiatric disorder. It is one of several conditions referred to as *mood disorders,* which are diagnosed based on the occurrence of periods of mood disruption. Understanding the concept of a mood episode is important for understanding mood disorders. A mood episode refers to a set of symptoms that occur during the same time period. This simple definition is made more complex because the set of symptoms used to make the diagnosis can include many different combinations of symptoms. For example, mood episodes can be understood much like an episode in a weekly television show. We can think of symptoms like the cast of characters. In this example, mood symptoms are the leading players, but to be recognizable as an episode of a specific show, the presence of other supporting actors is required. Although the entire cast may never be present in the same scene, and some actors may appear in more than one show, we can usually recognize a specific show by the appearance of any combination of a small number of cast members. Once we recognize the show, however, an episode can be said to

> *Bipolar disorder is also known as manic depression and is a common psychiatric disorder.*

continue for as long as the lead player and/or the supporting cast maintain a significant presence on the stage.

Most clinicians diagnose psychiatric problems by using a manual referred to as *DSM–IV–TR* (*Diagnostic and Statistical Manual*, 4th edition, text revision), which defines the symptom characteristics of each disorder. The *DSM–IV–TR* provides specific sets of symptoms that define episodes of depression, hypomania, mania, and mixed episodes. Throughout the rest of this chapter you will find an overview of the *DSM–IV–TR* concepts most likely to be used by your doctor.

What Is Mania?

Mania is more than just having a lot of energy or feeling great about yourself. Mania is a serious condition that is diagnosed when a person experiences several symptoms associated with an elevated or high mood that go beyond what most people experience. Mania includes symptoms such as increased energy, racing thoughts, inflated self-esteem, a decreased need for sleep, abnormal irritability, extreme happiness, poor judgment, and overparticipation in risky activities. These symptoms must be present during a period of least one week to be considered mania (see Table 2.1 for more details).

For many people, the initial symptoms of mania may feel pleasurable, however, an episode of abnormal mood elevation often causes serious disruption to an individual's normal life plans and goals. When mania causes an individual's thinking to be overly positive, judgment is impaired, actions are not evaluated adequately, and negative financial, career, or relationship consequences may follow. Mania often is associated with significant and sometimes severe problems in daily living. Sometimes the problems are so severe that a person must be hospitalized. Even when mania does not result in hospitalization, it may cause great upheavals in a person's life.

Table 2.1 Summary of DSM–IV–TR Episodes

Episode type	Predominant mood state	Duration	Associated features
Mania	High, happy, euphoric, expansive, irritable	At least one week	1. Increased self esteem/grandiosity 2. Decreased need for sleep 3. More talkative 4. Racing thought/flight of ideas 5. Distractible 6. Increased goal-directed activities/psychomotor agitation 7. Risk-taking
Hypomania	High, happy, euphoric, expansive, irritable	At least four days	1. Increased self-esteem/grandiosity 2. Decreased need for sleep 3. More talkative 4. Racing thoughts/flight of ideas 5. Distractible 6. Increased goal-directed activities/psychomotor agitation 7. Risk-taking
Depression	Low, sad, disinterested	At least two weeks	1. Sleep disturbance 2. Diminished interest 3. Guilt/low self-esteem 4. Decreased energy 5. Inability to concentrate/make simple decisions 6. Appetite disturbance 7. Psychomotor retardation/agitation 8. Suicidal ideation/morbid preoccupation
Mixed	High, happy, euphoric, expansive, irritable, low, sad, disinterested	At least one week	Associated features present that fulfill both mania and depression.

What Is Hypomania?

The term *hypomania* refers to a clearly abnormal mood state with mild to severe symptoms of mania that may last for a few days or may persist for many months. The key differences between mania and hypomania are both the severity of symptoms and, more importantly, the effect the symptoms have on your life (see Table 2.1 for more details). Mania can cause enormous problems in daily functioning and often leads to serious problems with a person's relationships or work functioning.

By definition, hypomania does not cause problems to the same extent as mania, and for some patients hypomania can be a pleasant state of good humor and high productivity. Unfortunately, for most people hypomania can be problematic. Things said and done during a hypomanic episode often have negative long-term consequences. For example, during a hypomanic episode, buying more clothes than necessary might delay rent or mortgage payments, or telling off-color jokes might bring attention at the office party but lessen the chances for promotion in the long run. Hypomania often occurs just before or immediately after other severe mood states. A hypomanic phase can be coupled with full manic episodes or it can occur at the beginning or end of a severe depression. In other words, a hypomanic episode may be a sign that a more severe manic episode is on the way, or it may be a sign that a person is going to "crash" and become depressed.

What Is Depression?

An episode of major depression, often simply referred to as *depression* is more than just the sad mood most people might experience when they have had a bad day. Major depression is a medical disorder that lasts at least two weeks and produces a combination of physical and emotional symptoms that make it very difficult to function in life (see Table 2.1 for more details).

At the heart of clinical depression is a loss of pleasure in activities that used to be fun or exciting. Also, people often have feelings of sadness, hopelessness, and pessimism. These symptoms are accompanied by a wide variety of physical symptoms such as difficulty sleeping, poor concentration and memory, low energy, and change in appetite. Not everyone will experience all of these physical symptoms. For example, someone may have problems with their sleep and feel low in energy, but their appetite may remain normal. Depression also changes the way a person thinks about the world. For example, it is not uncommon for people who are depressed to feel helpless and hopeless about their life situation, and, at times, people may feel that suicide is a rational alternative to their current situation (see Chapter 8). Because of the way in which a low mood can influence memory, people who are depressed may have a hard time remembering times when things went well, and may have a hard time imagining things going well in the future. Also, when depressed, it may be difficult to remember that depression is treatable.

Unipolar and Bipolar Mood Disorders

The *DSM–IV–TR* classifies mood disorders into two main types, unipolar and bipolar, which are based largely on which types of episodes have been diagnosed. Although unipolar and bipolar disorders are both considered mood disorders, they are different illnesses. Patients are diagnosed with unipolar disorders if they have only experienced episodes of depressed mood. They never experience the manic or hypomanic symptoms of bipolar disorder.

Subtypes of Bipolar Disorder

There are four subtypes of bipolar disorder: Bipolar I, Bipolar II, Cyclothymia, and Bipolar NOS (not otherwise specified).

Bipolar I refers to a condition in which patients have experienced one or more episodes of mania (see Table 2.2 for more details).

Although you do not need an episode of depression to get a diagnosis of Bipolar I, most people who have Bipolar I experience episodes of both mania and depression. In other words, most patients who have Bipolar I will have episodes of both depression and mania, while a few patients will have episodes of mania alone.

Bipolar II refers to a condition in which patients have had at least one hypomanic episode (see Table 2.2 for more details) but have never experienced a full manic episode. To meet criteria for Bipolar II, a patient also must have had at least one episode

Table 2.2 *Summary of Unipolar and Bipolar Disorders*

	Mania	*Hypomania*	*Depression*
Unipolar disorders			
Major depression	No	No	Yes
Dysthymic disorder	No	No	No, but person feels chronically sad or down
Bipolar disorders			
Bipolar I	Yes	Yes	Usually
Bipolar II	No	Yes	Yes
Cyclothymia	No	Yes	No, but person has periods where they feel sad or down
Bipolar NOS or	No	Yes	Person has some symptoms of depression
Bipolar NOS	No	Person has some symptoms of hypomania	Yes

of depression. More than 10 million men and women in the United States have bipolar disorder.

The major difference between Bipolar I and Bipolar II disorders is that Bipolar I requires at least one manic episode, whereas Bipolar II requires that periods of mood elevation meet criteria for hypomania but not necessarily the full criteria for mania. Table 2.2 may help you further understand these distinctions.

Cyclothymia refers to forms of bipolar illness that include a period of chronic mood instability (one year for children or adolescents, two years for adults). For the majority of the days during this period, patients experience abnormal mood states that must include frequent hypomanic symptoms that never meet full criteria for mania or major depression.

Bipolar NOS (not otherwise specified) refers to periods of clearly abnormal mood elevation that fail to meet criteria for any of the other subtypes. For example, a person can have some symptoms of mood elevation followed by an episode of depression. Because the symptoms of hypomania were too brief or too few to meet the full criteria for hypomania, the person would not qualify for Bipolar II but would qualify for a diagnosis of Bipolar NOS. Also a person with 4 or even 10 hypomanias but no depressions would be diagnosed as Bipolar NOS. Bipolar NOS is sometimes referred to as Atypical Bipolar disorder.

In summary, what distinguishes bipolar disorders from unipolar disorders is the occurrence of episodes of abnormally high, expansive, or irritable mood episodes (e.g., hypomania or mania). Episodes of depression (low mood) are also a common feature of bipolar disorder. A person with bipolar disorder may experience mood swings from excessive highs (mania) to profound hopelessness (depression), usually with periods of normal mood in between. Some individuals experience mixed episodes in which symptoms of both mania and depression occur at the same time.

How Common Is Bipolar Disorder?

Approximately 1%–5% of adults in the population have bipolar disorder. In the United States alone, more than 10 million people have bipolar disorder. Overall, the disorder affects both women and men equally. Bipolar disorder also affects adolescents and children; information on managing the disorder in this age range is provided in Chapter 6.

What Is the Course of the Disorder?

Bipolar disorder can occur at any time but usually begins before age 35. People between the ages of 15–25 have the highest risk of developing this disorder. However, the delay between the first signs and symptoms of the disorder and proper diagnosis and treatment is often 10 years.

The type, severity, and duration of mood episodes can vary. For example, some individuals may have more manic episodes or more depressed episodes, whereas others may have an equal number of depressive and manic episodes. The length of time that someone is in a normal mood state after an episode also can vary greatly. Without treatment, patients can experience shorter periods of normal mood and more periods of depression, hypomania, and mania. For most patients this increase in mood episodes ends after three to five episodes. During a 10-year period, the average bipolar patient will have about four mood episodes.

Approximately one out of eight individuals with bipolar disorder suffer from the *rapid cycling* form of the disorder (i.e., four or more mood episodes per year). Rapid cycling tends to be more common in women than in men. If a woman experiences an episode of bipolar disorder within four weeks after childbirth, that episode can be designated as having a postpartum onset. Some people also experience a seasonal pattern to bipolar disorder, where most episodes start and end around the same time each year.

Even among patients who have frequent severe episodes, there may be long periods of a normal mood state. Some doctors, patients, and family members may be tempted to interpret these periods of wellness as evidence that the diagnosis of bipolar disorder was incorrect. Unfortunately, this is seldom the case. Bipolar disorder often has natural periods of remission, but those who meet criteria for bipolar disorder will almost always relapse without treatment.

What Causes Bipolar Disorder?

Bipolar disorder is likely caused by multiple factors that interact with each other. It often runs in families and there is a genetic component to the disorder. For example, your chances of getting bipolar disorder are higher if your parents or siblings have this disorder. However, even though someone may have inherited the genes for bipolar disorder, there is no guarantee that this person will develop the disorder. A stressful environment or negative life events may interact with an underlying genetic or biological vulnerability to produce the disorder. In other words, some people are born with genes that make it more likely that they will get bipolar disorder. It is not known why some people with these genes develop bipolar disorder and others do not. Often, a stressful event seems to trigger the first episode. Therefore, an individual's coping skills or style for handling stress also may play a role in the development of symptoms. In some cases, drug abuse (e.g., alcohol, amphetamines, LSD, cocaine, etc.) can trigger the disorder. Stressful life events also may lead to a loss of sleep or a change in usual routines. Such changes in one's schedule can contribute to the onset and recurrence of depression and mania.

Comorbidity

Comorbidity is a psychiatric term that refers to a situation in which a person has two or more psychiatric disorders that often occur at the same time. The *DSM–IV* lists more than 330 different types of psychiatric disorders. A person with bipolar disorder is very likely to meet the criteria for one or more additional disorders. No one knows why, but having bipolar disorder appears to make you more vulnerable to anxiety disorders, alcoholism, substance abuse, bulimia, attention deficit disorder, and migraine headaches. Successful treatment of bipolar disorder almost always improves these other conditions. Likewise, successful treatment of these conditions usually improves the symptoms of bipolar disorder. Unfortunately for some patients, the treatments for other disorders can worsen symptoms of bipolar disorder. For example, the medicines used to treat obsessive-compulsive disorder (antidepressants) and attention deficit disorder (stimulants) may worsen symptoms of bipolar disorder and even cause a manic

Table 2.3 *Protective and Risk Factors in Bipolar Disorder*

Protective factors	Risk factors

▪ Use of mood stabilizing medications
▪ Abstinence from alcohol
▪ Abstinence from recreational drug use
▪ Structured schedule
  ▪ Regular awake and sleep times
  ▪ Schedule of recurring social activity
▪ Support system
  ▪ Professionals
  ▪ Family
  ▪ Friends
▪ Psychotherapy
	▪ Alcohol
	▪ Recreational drugs
	▪ Abrupt discontinuation of medications
	  ▪ Mood stabilizers
	  ▪ Antidepressants
	  ▪ Anxiolytics
	▪ Sleep disruption
	▪ Loss of supports
	▪ Distorted thinking patterns
	▪ Interpersonal conflict
	▪ Role transition
	▪ Negative emotional communications
	▪ East–west travel
	▪ Anxiety disorders and stress

episode. When this happens it is usually possible to find other treatments that help these conditions.

Factors in Coping with Bipolar Disorder

Some of the strategies that protect you from future episodes include: taking medications appropriately; using social, family, and community supports; using communication or problem-solving skills; and utilizing treatment resources such as psychotherapy. Throughout this book we will present strategies that utilize these protective factors while avoiding risk factors (see Table 2.3 for a list of protective versus risk factors).

3

Medication Names and Common Dosages

This chapter reviews the medications commonly used to treat bipolar disorder. As an active participant in your treatment, it is important for you to know the purpose as well as the proper dosage, side effects, and schedule for each medication you use. This information makes it easier for you and your doctor to select and adjust medications in a manner that most benefits you. Please discuss your concerns about medication with your physician. Your doctor will be able to help you cope with the side effects or consider alternative treatments.

> *If you have bipolar disorder, it is important that you know the proper dosage and potential side effects of your medication.*

Do I Really Need to Take Medications?

Many individuals have mixed feelings about taking medications, and, in an ideal world, most people would choose not to do so. However, numerous studies have shown the benefit of medications for treating episodes of depression and mania and helping to prevent new episodes. Medications, such as those referred to as mood stabilizers and antidepressants, can be thought of as tools that may help you feel better and help you take control of your life.

What Types of Medications are Used to Treat Bipolar Disorder?

The following sections describe the four major types of medications used to treat bipolar disorder: mood stabilizers, antidepressants, antipsychotics, and antianxiety (anxiolytics). These medications are the main tools for controlling bipolar disorder. Used individually or in combination, these medications provide a way for you to manage your bipolar disorder. Other medication tools also may be used to treat additional symptoms.

Before we describe in more detail the types of medication, their purposes, and some side effects, we should first provide some important information about the *names* of these classes of medication.

Drugs often are classified according to the purpose for which they *first* got regulatory approval in the United States. Although many drugs are found to have a variety of uses in addition to this first use, the original classification sticks. This can be confusing, because doctors often prescribe drugs classified as *antidepressants* to treat anxiety and drugs called *anxiolytics* to treat insomnia. For this reason, it is extremely important for you to know the purpose for which a medication is precribed, not just its classification. It helps to try to have a sense of humor with the well-meaning people who may question your medications because they take these classification terms at face value. For example, a family member may wonder why you are taking a medication for anxiety when you have bipolar disorder. Similar questions about your medication may arise when you pick up your medications at the pharmacy, when you share the names of the medications with your friends or family, or even when you see your primary care physician. When this happens, as with any questions that might arise about your medication, speak to your doctor before you make any changes.

Mood Stabilizers

The goal of treatment with mood stabilizers is to keep your mood within a normal range. While experts often use the term mood to refer to treatments for bipolar disorder, the term *mood stabilizer* is not a precisely defined scientific term. There is general agreement among experts that lithium (e.g., Eskalith and Lithobid), valproate (Depakote), lamotrigine (e.g., Lamictal), carbamazepine (Tegretol), and olanazpine (Zyprexa) are mood stabilizers. Each of these drugs has been shown to be an effective treatment for mania and/or relapse prevention in two or more rigorous studies. There are numerous studies showing that lithium is effective for preventing relapse and for the treatment of bipolar depression. Two studies have shown lamotrigine can be effective for treatment of bipolar depression and two have shown benefit for relapse prevention, particularly for prevention of depressive recurrence. Olanzapine has demonstrated excellent benefits against acute mania, has some antidepressant benefit, and appears to be particularly useful for preventing manic relapse. Quetiapine has gained approval for the treatment of acute bipolar depression, mania and relapse prevention. Ariprazole has approval for treatment of acute mania and prevention of manic relapse. Ziprasidone has approval for acute mania and maintence treatment.

Other drugs may also possess mood-stabilizing properties. It seems reasonable to refer to a drug as a mood stabilizer or a possible mood stabilizer if the drug: (1) works as a treatment for mania, depression, or as a prevention of relapse; and (2) does not increase a patient's rate of mood cycling or cause a switch from one abnormal mood state to another. Medications sometimes used by experts as mood stabilizers include calcium channel blockers like verapamil (Calan, Isoptin), oxcarbazepine (Trileptal), and Omega-3 fatty acids, but these are generally regarded as unproven innovative options. None of these have yet proven benefit in a rigorous study or been granted FDA approval for treatment of any aspect of bipolar disorder.

All medications can cause side effects. The goal is for you to work with your physician to find a mood stabilizer that best protects you or helps you recover from episodes of depression or mania, without giving you side effects that are too bothersome.

> *All medications can cause side effects.*

Antidepressants

It is fairly common for physicians to prescribe antidepressants approved for treatment of unipolar depression to treat depressive episodes associated with bipolar disorder. However, this use is controversial and not approved by the FDA. The best available evidence shows little benefit or harm when these antidepressants were added to ongoing treatment with mood stabilizers to treat bipolar depression. Even so, use of antidepressants should be carefully monitored to determine whether these medications provide benefit or actually worsen the course of bipolar illness. Some depressed bipolar patients will switch from depression to mania whether or not they are treated with standard antidepressant medication. Currently, experts disagree about the extent to which antidepressant medications increase the rate of switch above what would be expected spontaneously. In other words, the antidepressant tool, while possibly useful for controlling depression in some patients, may result in raising mood state above normal and cause a person to become manic or hypomanic. In addition, some bipolar patients who take antidepressants experience a worsening of their depression or more depressive episodes. Much more likely than either of these outcomes is the probability that bipolar patients will get no extra benefit from an antidepressant than they get by taking a mood stabilizer alone. For this reason, open communication and regular follow-up with your physician are necessary to be sure you are not being made worse off by your treatment. Your physician will monitor you for the emergence of manic symptoms, but he or she can do a much better job with assistance from you and other members of your support team.

Talk to your physician about how you are feeling. If you notice difficulty sleeping, excessive energy, irritability, restlessness, excessive talkativeness, racing thoughts, or a sense of agitation/restlessness during your antidepressant treatment, make sure you report these symptoms to your care providers immediately.

Although a low level of mood elevation may be enjoyable, you do not want these symptoms to escalate into mania. Remember that mania is characterized as a disorder because of the problems it causes in your life. To keep control of your life and your ability to seek and follow your goals, report any early symptoms of mania or hypomania to your physician. With monitoring and care, antidepressant medication can be a valuable addition to your toolbox for treating your bipolar depression.

Table 3.1 provides a list of antidepressant medications. You will note that Wellbutrin-SR and Paxil are listed first because these medications are believed to be less likely to cause mania than some older antidepressant medications.

Antipsychotics

Antipsychotics were first developed as treatment for the hallucinations and delusions caused by schizophrenia. However, antipsychotic medications have been shown to have specific antimanic effects even in manic patients who don't have any symptoms of psychosis. Antipsychotics are frequently prescribed in the context of a manic episode and may be especially helpful in clearing up disorganized or distorted thinking, as well as hallucinations.

A common property of antipsychotic drugs is the ability to block receptors for the chemical, or neurotransmitter, called dopamine.

Table 3.1 *Common Medications for Bipolar Disorder: Antidepressants*

Generic name	Trade name	Common starting daily dose	Common daily dose range
Antidepressants			
Bupropion	Wellbutrin-XR	100 mg	300 mg
Paroxetine	Paxil	10–20 mg	20 mg
Sertraline	Zoloft	50 mg	50–200 mg
Fluvoxamine	Luvox	25–50 mg	150–300 mg
Fluoxetine	Prozac	20 mg	20–60 mg
Citalopram	Celexa	20 mg	20–40 mg
Escitalopram	Lexapro	10 mg	10–40 mg
Venlafaxine	Effexor	25–37.5 mg	75–150 mg
Mirtazapine	Remeron	15 mg	15–60 mg
Trazodone	Desyrel	50 mg	300–600 mg
Phenelzine	Nardil	15 mg	60–90 mg
Tranylcypromine	Parnate	10 mg	30–40 mg

Too much dopamine in your brain may contribute to some of the symptoms of mania. You may hear some of your physicians use the term *neuroleptics*. These medications are the same as antipsychotics. Older drugs such as chlorpromazine (Thorazine), thioridazine (Mellaril), perphenazine (Trilafon), haloperidol (Haldol), or thioxixene (Navane) are dopamine receptor blockers. As a class, neuroleptics are considered helpful for acute mania, but their usefulness is often limited by side effects. Early in the course of treatment, patients treated with neuroleptics may experience muscle stiffness, tremors, and sometimes restlessness. Long-term use of neuroleptic drugs is associated with potentially irreversible movement disorders such as tardive dyskinesia (TD), a disorder characterized by repetitive, involuntary, purposeless movements.

Newer antipsychotics are now available for your physician to use to treat mania. Clozapine was the first member of a new class of antipsychotics sometimes called atypical antipsychotic medications. Although many experts consider clozapine to be a highly effective treatment, the studies necessary for FDA approval have not been done. This class of medications also includes six members that have been approved by the FDA for acute mania: risperidone (Risperdal), olanzapine (Zyprexa), quetiapine (Seroquel), ziprasidone (Geodon), aripiprazole (Abilify), and asenapine (Saphris). Similar to the older drugs, these newer drugs also block dopamine receptors but with much less potency than the older neuroleptic medications. The atypical antipsychotics also block some receptors for a neurotransmitter called serotonin. Drugs with this combination of low potency dopamine blockade and serotonin blockade are much less likely to cause the kind of intolerable side effects seen with older neuroleptics. The atypical antipsychotics are frequently used alone or in combination with mood stabilizers for the treatment of acute mania.

After recovery from a manic episode, it is common practice to decrease the dosages of antipsychotic medications. However, some patients begin to have manic symptoms soon after the dosages of antipsychotic medication are lowered. These patients and others for whom risk of manic recurrence is high may be prescribed antipsychotics on a continual basis to keep mania from coming back. Consequently, antipsychotics can be thought of as a medication for both the immediate treatment of mania and for the prevention of manic or psychotic symptoms.

Anxiolytic (Antianxiety) Medications

Anxiety is a problem for many patients with bipolar disorder apart from their mood episodes. Even for those patients without anxiety problems between episodes, anxiety symptoms very frequently accompany episodes of depression or mania. In addition, sleep problems are common in depression, hypomania, and mania. Within the anxiolytic class, the most frequently used medications are benzodiazepines. These medications include lorazepam (Ativan), clonazepam

Table 3.2 *Common Medications for Bipolar Disorder: Mood Stabilizers*

Generic name	Trade name	Common starting daily dose	Common daily dose range
Mood stabilizers			
Lithium Carbonate	Lithobid/ Eskalith/ Lithonate	600 mg	900–2400 mg
Carbamazepine	Tegretol	400 mg	200–1600 mg
Divalproex	Depakote	750 mg	750–2750 mg
Lamotrigine	Lamictal	12.5*–25 mg	50–400 mg
Olanzapine	Zyprexa	5–15 mg	2.5–20 mg
Quetiapine	Seroquel	100 mg	300–600 mg
Aripripazole	Abilify	5–15 mg	5–30 mg
Ziprasidone	Geodon	80 mg	80–240 mg
Possible mood stabilizers			
Oxcarbazepine	Trileptal	150 mg	450–900 mg
Verapamil	Calan	120 mg	120–360 mg
Amlodipine	Norvasc	2.5 mg	2.5–10 mg
Omega-3 fatty acid	(many available)	1,000 mg	3,000–12,000 mg
Inositol	(many available)	5,000 mg	5000–30,000 mg

* Common starting dose for Lamotrigine is 12.5 mg if you also are taking Divalproex, but 25 mg if not prescribed Divalproex.

(Klonopin), diazepam (Valium), and alprazolam (Xanax), and they are used to help treat anxiety and sleeplessness in bipolar disorder. In addition, the benzodiazepines may be used to help control some of the early symptoms of hypomania. All benzodiazepines have the potential to cause physical and psychological dependence or addiction. The potential for abuse seems to be greatest with drugs that produce a quick effect and that are quickly removed from your blood stream, such as alprazolam (Xanax). The potential for abuse seems to be least with benzodiazepines that have a slower effect and spend a longer time in your blood stream, such as clonazepam (Klonopin).

Most standard antidepressant medications appear to have excellent effects on reducing anxiety, but they require several weeks of consistent use to become effective and may cause worsening of bipolar disorder in some patients.

> *All benzodiazepines have the potential to cause physical and psychological dependence or addiction*

Finding the Correct Dose

Effective treatment depends on finding the correct dose of medication. Finding the right dose for you becomes easier if you take your medications as directed by your doctor and keep him or her informed about your response to the medications. Tables 3.1, 3.2, and 3.3 provide you with some information and dosage ranges on common mood stabilizers, antidepressants, and antipsychotics. Your physician may prescribe dosages outside of these ranges. These ranges are displayed to give you a frame of reference and to help you take an active role in discussing dosages with your doctor.

Table 3.3 *Common Medications for Bipolar Disorder: Antipsychotics*

Generic name	Trade name	Common starting daily dose	Common daily dose range
Antipsychotics			
Clozapine	Clozaril	25 mg	25–400 mg
Risperidone	Risperdal	1.0 mg	0.5–6 mg
Olanzapine	Zyprexa	5–10 mg	2.5–20 mg
Quetiapine	Seroquel	100 mg	25–800 mg
Ziprasidone	Geodon	80 mg	80–240 mg
Aripiprazole	Abilify	5–15 mg	5–30 mg
Asenapine	Saphris	10 mg	10–20 mg
Trifluoperazine	Stelazine	2–5 mg	5–10 mg
Perphenazine	Trilafon	4 mg	4–32 mg
Haloperidol	Haldol	2 mg	0.5–10 mg

4

Getting in the Habit of Taking Medications

Finding a Reliable Way to Take Your Medications

It is important that you develop a habit of taking your pills regularly. Taking your medications at regular times during the day and using common daily events to remind you to take your pills are useful strategies to help keep your medication plan on track. For example, you may place your morning dose in the bathroom so that when you are brushing your teeth in the morning you see and remember to take your pills. Because midday doses are particularly hard to remember, you will want to develop a way to link taking your medication with another well-established habit in your life such as eating lunch. With repeated practice, taking the lunchtime dose becomes as automatic as eating your meal.

One reason you may miss a dose is that you may forget to take your pills with you before you leave your home. Many patients cope with this by keeping a small supply of pills (enough for three days) in different places (for example, a separate container of pills in a desk drawer, luggage, or knapsack). Keeping back-up pills in your travel bags makes it that much harder to leave for a vacation or business trip without your pills.

It is also important that you communicate the importance of medication treatment to your family members. At times, family members may be unaware of the beneficial effects of the medication and may be frightened by the idea that you are taking medicine. Some well-meaning family members or friends may want you to *just get better* and may end up encouraging you to skip your treatment or to miss a clinic appointment. Family and friends often do this out of an understandable desire to see you as recovered or not really ill in the first place. Unfortunately, this seldom leads to any benefit and usually has the unfavorable effect of increasing the likelihood of worsening symptoms or a relapse.

To help prevent these outcomes and reduce negative pressures on you, we invite you to have your family members or other support persons read this chapter, as well as the rest of this book. We also believe that it would be beneficial for you to discuss with them how they can support you in keeping on schedule with your medications or your office visits.

Finally, remember to keep track of the amount of pills that you have left in your bottle. This way you can ask your doctor for refills or you can pick up your refills before you run out of medication. Remember that medications are a useful tool to help you maintain your mood within the range you want, so that you can best pursue your life goals. These tools are only useful if you use them the right way.

Consistent Use of Your Medication

For many individuals, a combination of medications may be used to enhance mood stability. Once your mood stabilizes, there is often the temptation to discontinue medication and to believe that the disorder has been cured. Unfortunately, bipolar disorder is a lifelong condition, one that requires ongoing treatment. We use the analogy of a seatbelt to help underscore the importance of this point. As you know, a seatbelt is a protective device designed to prevent injury in the case of a car accident. Hopefully, that accident never happens, but if it does, you are prepared. In a similar way, taking medications for bipolar disorder protects you from depression and mania. Even when your symptoms feel completely under control, it is important to take your medications regularly.

At times, you may miss some of the highs that go with a hypo-manic mood. However, remember that the goal of taking the pills is to keep you in control of your life. Manic episodes take away that control and the ability for you to plan your life the way you want. Be careful of sacrificing your life goals for a desire to feel high. First, use medications to help you stay in control, and then figure out how to make life as fun and fulfilling as possible.

> *Even when your symptoms feel completely under control, it is important to take your medications regularly*

The self-guided care box on page 30 is designed to provide you with opportunities to think through and clarify your goals for using medications as tools to help control your bipolar disorder. Writing out your responses will help you better articulate your reasons and will also provide you with a written record for review at a later time.

Coping with Medication Side Effects

Medication side effects are difficult, but you are not alone with this struggle. If you are experiencing bothersome side effects, schedule a meeting with your psychiatrist or therapist to discuss ways of coping with these symptoms. In response to your side effects, you and your physician may determine that it is necessary to discontinue a particular medication. Most often, adjusting the dose or the time the medication is taken makes it possible to tolerate the medicine long enough to get whatever benefit it has to offer. Side effects tend to be most difficult just after a medication is added, but tend to gradually subside over time. However, sometimes side effects will remain bothersome to you and the best course of action may be to continue the medication despite the side effects. In that case, you and your treatment team may add coping skills to reduce the impact of these side effects on your life.

Self-Guided Care: Motivation for Medication Use

I wish to use medications regularly for my benefit, to help return my moods to the normal range, or to help protect me against a future mood episode. When I am feeling better, I may have some urges to quit my medications. At those times, it will be important for me to remember why I want to continue my medications. Medication is used to protect me against the following effects of depression and mania.

Manic symptoms and life-consequences I want to avoid:

1.

2.

3.

Depression symptoms and life-consequences I want to avoid:

1.

2.

3.

A few reminders I want to use to help me stay motivated for medication use:

1 .

2.

3.

The most important thing to remember is to stay in treatment and to discuss your concerns with your doctor when you have side effects. It is important that you do not let the side effects deter you from taking your medication. Instead, be active. Work with your treatment team to solve side-effect problems. Time spent finding the medication that works for you is time well spent.

Medication Monitoring

Work with your treatment team to solve side-effect problems.

Monitoring your medication is a good idea to help ensure that you continue to take your medications as prescribed. This is part of making sure that you use the tools that you and your treatment team have selected in the best manner. Chapter 12 provides a form for monitoring your moods and activities to maximize your daily control over your disorder. This form also includes a place to record your use of medications. Research has found that even this simple extra attention to monitoring pill taking helps people stay on track with their daily use of medication. With a little practice at linking pill taking to daily routines, and regular monitoring of moods and medication use, you can maximize the value that medications can have in helping control your bipolar disorder.

Medications and Pregnancy

Women with bipolar disorder who want to have children should work very closely with family support and health care providers when thinking about conceiving. Careful planning and being well-informed are the keys to successful management of bipolar illness during and after pregnancy. Careful planning can help you best manage bipolar disorder by minimizing symptoms and avoiding risks to your unborn child. First, it is important to never stop taking medications before talking with your prescribing doctor. You also shouldn't make sudden changes to your medication as you consider conception or during pregnancy. Such changes might lead to major side effects, risks to the fetus, and increase your risk for a mood episode. Second, more information than ever is available on medications used to treat bipolar disorder and their impact on the fetus. Contact and carefully plan with your physician which medications provide you with the best balance of mood stabilization and safety for your baby during pregnancy. This planning should include discussions with your clinician prior to initiating conception, discussions during the course of pregnancy, and planning for the postpartum and nursing phases of having a child.

Psychotherapy for Bipolar Disorder

This book is designed to provide you and members of your support network with basic information about bipolar disorder and its management. Each of the chapters focuses on a different element of functioning that may influence the course of bipolar disorder. These topic areas—information about the disorder, medication use and compliance, stress and schedule management, thinking biases, relationships, communication skills, problem solving, and construction of a treatment contract—are the same topic areas that typically receive attention in psychotherapy. Psychotherapy provides a chance to get more help with these or other topics that are relevant for individuals with bipolar disorder.

When you choose psychotherapy, it is important to find a therapist who is knowledgeable about bipolar disorder and with whom you are comfortable talking. A good therapist can be a crucial addition to your treatment team.

When choosing a therapist, you and your family need to be smart shoppers. Talk with the therapist about his or her approach to treating bipolar disorder, including the therapist's expectations regarding the length of treatment and when you should first expect to see benefits. Also ask for the therapist's expectations of you and how you can make the best use of psychotherapy.

> *A good therapist can be a crucial addition to your treatment team.*

Psychotherapy can play an important role in helping you manage bipolar disorder. At any time you may supplement the information and strategies introduced in this book with the more specific help that can be provided by a therapist. In all cases, remember that you are the primary consumer of treatment. Always act as an informed caregiver to yourself and pull together a treatment team that can provide you with the best benefit.

Specific Psychotherapies for Bipolar Disorder

The past decade has brought welcome research attention to how psychotherapy can help in the management of bipolar disorder. To date, three types of psychotherapy have received prominent attention in research studies: family focused therapy, interpersonal psychotherapy, and cognitive-behavior therapy. There is evidence that these therapies can treat bipolar depression and protect against relapse, and, for people on mood stabilizers, may offer more powerful effects than antidepressant medications. We want you to know the brand name of these therapies because they may help you identify therapists who have specialized in the treatment of bipolar disorder and who have adopted a treatment style that has been examined by research. However, it is also important to know that these three types of psychotherapy share many of the same elements of treatment. That is, even though the originators of these treatments come from different theoretical traditions, the elements of treatment they emphasize are very similar. We find this comforting and believe it reflects a shared understanding of what is important for the management of bipolar disorder.

Family focused therapy (FFT) is oriented toward seeing the individual with bipolar disorder together with her or his family. It emphasizes education about the nature of the disorder combined with active work in providing better communication patterns within the family and in developing an active problem-solving style for the challenges brought by bipolar disorder. Individuals and family members in treatment can expect direct attention to the mood episodes that define the disorder, but also attention to how everyday emotions are perceived and handled within the family, with a goal of promoting understanding, good communication, and wellbeing for all family members. A focus on education and communication patterns is also at the heart of *interpersonal psychotherapy* (IPT), a therapy that directs attention to the interpersonal conflicts and role challenges that are associated with mood disorders. The focused approach on interpersonal issues helps ensure a problem-focused way to resolve some of these issues. For the management of bipolar disorder, this treatment also explicitly includes a focus on managing activities and sleep/wake cycles to try to reduce the ways in which these cycles affect mood episodes. *Cognitive-behavior therapy* (CBT) also includes this focus on managing activity levels in relation to long-term goals, enhancing communication and problem solving, enhancing stress management, and helping manage the negative or overpositive thinking patterns that play a role in maintaining or exacerbating mood episodes. For all of these treatments, there is also attention to the symptoms that may signal that a mood episode is likely, with the therapist working with the individual with bipolar disorder to intervene early to reduce the likelihood of a full episode.

All of these types of treatments share the idea that therapy should be an active process for both the therapist and the patient. These are not therapies where you do all the talking and receive no guidance. In each of these therapies, the therapist is there to share her or his knowledge of the disorder and practical strategies for managing mood episodes and reducing the impact of bipolar disorder on your life and your goals. For this reason, we want you to be very active in talking with a potential new therapist about his or her approach and what can be expected from therapy. Research has provided some guidance on the elements of therapy that can be helpful in changing the course of the disorder, and we want you to be active in trying to seek out these elements of treatment and finding a therapist with whom you feel comfortable and confident.

Selecting a Therapist

When you or a family member has bipolar disorder, it is very important to be an especially good consumer when it comes to selecting a therapist. Your physician may give you one or two names of therapists for you to consider, or you may have a list of therapists provided by your insurance company–these are the therapists the insurance company has contracted with for providing service to your insurance plan. You may be able to see a therapist who is not on the list provided by your insurance plan, but you may only receive partial coverage for these visits and have to pay more of the costs of therapy out of pocket. We understand that you may need to be sensitive to the costs of therapy, but also encourage you to select a therapist who is specifically knowledgeable about bipolar disorder. To find the right therapist, you will have to be a good consumer and detective and consider asking your physician about the skills and style of therapy of the therapists in your area, asking others (friends or family members who have been in therapy) and interviewing the therapist directly, before entering into ongoing therapy. When inquiring about the therapist's skills and knowledge about bipolar disorder, we recommend you ask the following questions.

1. Does the therapist have experience and skill in working specifically with individuals with bipolar disorder?

2. What type of care does the therapist offer; is she or he skilled with the types of therapies found to be helpful in scientific studies (e.g., CBT, FFT, or IPT)?
3. How active is the therapist in providing patients with information on bipolar disorder and in working on specific strategies to try to reduce the frequency, duration, and severity of episodes?

By asking these questions, you are hoping to find that the therapist is knowledgeable about bipolar disorder and the importance of working to prevent relapses as well as treating a current mood episode. By understanding the nature of bipolar disorder, the importance of mood stabilizing medication, and the role of interpersonal and other life stress in the course of bipolar disorder, this therapist may be best suited to consider the range of treatment options to help you meet your personal goals. In many cases, this treatment will involve active discussions or practice of various skills to manage bipolar disorder and mood episodes. These include ways to reduce stress, enhance problem solving, improve communication, or change thinking and activity patterns. This treatment may be delivered in individual therapy sessions or in group treatment. General supportive therapy may also be of value in providing information, guiding your decision making, and including you as part of a team in managing the challenges of bipolar disorder. Though supportive therapy can be helpful, it is very important for you to seek a therapist who can truly be a knowledgeable guide about ways to manage the mood changes and interpersonal challenges that bipolar disorder brings to the lives of patients and their families. We also want you to feel good about your therapist, and how she or he treats you. After a first meeting you will want to evaluate whether you felt good about how the therapist treated you and your questions and whether the therapist is both caring and respectful of you. Having confidence in and feeling cared about by your prospective therapist is an important part of the decision process. You will not make a final decision after just one meeting, but hopefully you will gain enough information to know whether you should also consider other options or continue with further visits with (and further evaluation of) this therapist.

Although it may seem awkward for you to "interview" a therapist before agreeing to working with them, we strongly recommend this approach. After all, many of us have sought out clear advice from friends before choosing a repair shop for your car (did they do a good job, are they experienced with fixing foreign cars, etc.). We want you to place at least as much attention on *your care* as you do on the care of your car! Be a good consumer; select a therapist that is caring and knowledgeable about bipolar disorder and the range of skills that can be used to better manage this disorder.

Bipolar Disorder in Adolescents and Children

Although there has been a lot of controversy about this diagnosis in children, there is increasing evidence that bipolar disorder can affect children. It is estimated that 1%–1.5% of children have bipolar disorder, and among adults with the disorder, one-third to one-half report that their mood episodes began during childhood or adolescence. The initial episode in children and adolescents is often depression, with onset of mood episodes occurring most frequently in later childhood or early adolescence, although anxiety and other emotional disturbances may be present much earlier. Because bipolar disorder is a genetic illness, the risks for bipolar disorder increase if family members have the disorder, particularly if both parents have the disorder (and may exceed a 50:50 chance).

How Does Bipolar Disorder Present in Children?

As with adults, children and adolescents with bipolar disorder can experience symptoms of mania, hypomania, and depression. However, there are important differences among adults and children and adolescents in the types of symptoms that are characteristic of mood episodes. For example, youth with bipolar disorder are more likely to have a form of the disorder that is chronic and rapid-cycling, with frequent, rapidly shifting episodes (sometimes even within the same day), and mixed episodes (with symptoms of both depression and mania). Youth are also more likely to present as extremely irritable with explosive outbursts.

During periods of depression, children can appear cranky, sad, whiny and clingy. As with adults, they may have decreased energy and decreased interest in activities (some parents describe that their child is more like a "couch potato" than usual). The child may see herself or himself negatively (describe themselves as stupid, bad, or ugly), feel negatively about their lives and their future (e.g., "things never work out for me"), have difficulty concentrating or making decisions, and be restless or physically slowed down. Children and adolescents may also have difficulty sleeping or may sleep more than usual and experience changes in their appetite. It is important to note that youth, even young children, can experience suicidal thoughts (e.g., "I wish I was dead"; "I wish I'd never been born"), as well as suicidal impulses and behaviors. If a child is reporting any of these thoughts and feelings, it is important to take them seriously and have them quickly evaluated by a professional.

Even young children can experience suicidal thoughts, impulses, and behaviors.

During periods of mania, children can appear very giddy, silly, high, and/or they may be extremely irritable and explosive. When irritable, they may have intense, long-lasting rages, which can be provoked by seemingly minor issues (or sometimes seem to come out of the blue). As in adult forms of the illness, children may display grandiosity (for example, thinking that they can fly; that they are the same as an adult), physical restlessness, and racing thoughts. They may talk very quickly, be more active (for example, doing more with friends, starting many new projects), and (less typically) require less sleep than usual. Children and adolescents may also behave in an impulsive or risky manner. Children and adolescents may be daredevils, and may display increased interest in sexual matters. During rages, youth may become verbally or physically aggressive, damage property, and appear out of control. More rarely, youth may experience psychotic symptoms, such as hearing voices, or having intense, unusual and unrealistic beliefs, called delusions.

Comorbidity

Youth with bipolar disorder often have other disorders as well. Recent research suggests that 60% or more have attention-deficit-hyperactivity disorder (ADHD). Many children with bipolar disorder also have other behavioral problems such as oppositional-defiant disorder (ODD) or conduct disorder. A significant percentage of children with bipolar disorder also have problems with anxiety, including excessive anxiety about being separated from parents, social anxiety, and excessive worry. These children may also be more likely to have learning or developmental disabilities.

What Is the Course of the Illness in Children?

At this time, the long-term course of bipolar disorder in children has not yet been determined. However, many adults with bipolar disorder report that their symptoms started in childhood or adolescence, suggesting that the disorder is continuous across development. The few studies that have followed children with bipolar disorder over time suggest that the disorder often follows a waxing and waning course. For example, recent short-term follow-up studies suggest that bipolar disorder in youth tends to be chronic, with long episodes and a high risk for relapse after remission.

How Does Bipolar Disorder Impact Children?

Children with bipolar disorder often experience difficulty at home, at school, and/or with peers. Some children with bipolar disorder function well at school but can be very disruptive at home. Because the child's moods and behaviors can be unpredictable, family members may feel stressed and anxious about the child's symptoms. For example, parents will sometimes report that they are walking on eggshells to avoid triggering an emotional explosion. There may also be significant conflict in the family associated with the child's oppositionality, aggression, and emotional instability. Children with bipolar disorder also may often exhibit anger and aggression toward their siblings and family pets.

Children with bipolar disorder can display a range of functioning at school. Some children do very well academically, socially, and emotionally in the structured setting of school. Some children experience minor difficulties. However, some children experience significant difficulty at school. They may be unable to remain focused and attentive, may feel groggy or tired because of medication, or have trouble sitting still during classes. They may also have difficulty regularly attending school or getting to school on time because of an inability to rouse in the morning. Many children and adolescents may feel exhausted or burnt out by the end of the school day, making it extremely difficult to complete homework assignments. Children may also exhibit behavioral problems at school and behave in a non-compliant or aggressive manner toward school staff. Taken together, these problems may significantly interfere with their ability to master academic material, successfully complete schoolwork, and enjoy school.

The transition from high school to college may be challenging for older adolescents with bipolar disorder. They may feel overwhelmed by the increased demands for independence and self-regulation. They may also become overwhelmed by the amount of schoolwork required. They may have trouble going to class regularly and completing work without the structure that they were used to in high school.

Emotionally, they may struggle with the added responsibilities of becoming an adult (e.g., paying bills and managing their own time).

Youth with bipolar disorder may also experience difficulty with peer relationships, including social isolation, teasing, and frequent conflict with other children. If they exhibit impulsive or aggressive behaviors, they may have difficulty making or sustaining friendships. Children and adolescents may miss social cues or misinterpret the intentions of others (e.g., thinking that other children are being mean when they are not) and may feel very anxious about interacting with others. They may also feel emotionally overwhelmed by social demands and may avoid or withdraw from peers.

How Is Childhood Bipolar Disorder Treated?

The first step to treating this disorder is to obtain a thorough evaluation. The evaluation should be made by a child psychiatrist or child psychologist with expertise in assessing and diagnosing mood disorders in children. The evaluation typically includes speaking with the parent(s), as well as interviewing and observing the child. The evaluation will include a review of the child's current symptoms, a review of his or her history and development, questions about family history, previous treatments, and medical history. Additional forms of assessment such as neuropsychological or psychological testing may be helpful in clarifying other areas of difficulty, although these tests cannot diagnose bipolar disorder.

Medications

As with adult bipolar disorder, medications are central to treating bipolar disorder in children and adolescents. The medications that are used in youth are the same ones that are typically prescribed to adults, including mood stabilizers (e.g., Depakote and lithium), and atypical antipsychotics (e.g., Risperdal, Seroquel, and Zyprexa). Although less is known about the effects of these medications in youth, research suggests that they can be very helpful in reducing mood symptoms, decreasing aggression, and improving functioning.

Additional medications such as stimulants or antidepressants may also be prescribed to address other symptoms or disorders that the child is experiencing. However, these medications are not typically prescribed until the child is on a mood stabilizing treatment and is more stable because these medications can sometimes exacerbate or bring on symptoms of bipolar disorder.

Psychotherapy

Although little is known about the effectiveness of psychotherapy for childhood bipolar disorder, it may be useful (with older children or adolescents) in helping youth learn about their disorder, address issues of self-esteem, and address issues of functioning. A specific form of therapy called cognitive-behavior therapy (CBT) may be used to target distorted thinking patterns, develop coping skills, address anxiety, and improve social skills. Among adolescents, therapy may also address strategies for decreasing high-risk behaviors such as alcohol or substance use and abuse.

Family therapy can be an especially important component of treatment. Parents may benefit from learning different ways of interacting and parenting children with bipolar disorder. They may also benefit from learning strategies to help children manage their mood symptoms, address behavior problems, and decrease stress and conflict in the family. Recent research suggests that family conflict and stress can precipitate relapse of bipolar disorder in adults and adolescents, suggesting that decreasing these problems may be important in managing bipolar symptoms. In addition, it is important for parents to obtain support because it can often be very stressful and isolating to have a child who is experiencing this illness. Finally, siblings may benefit from the opportunity to learn about bipolar disorder and talk about their concerns.

School Supports for Children with Bipolar Disorder

Many children and adolescents with bipolar disorder may benefit from additional supports or accommodations at school. Because bipolar disorder is considered a disability under federal law, some children and adolescents with bipolar disorder may qualify for special education services and be eligible for an Individualized Education Plan (IEP). Alternatively, children may be eligible to receive accommodations under a Section 504 plan. Because it can be tricky to navigate the special education system, it is important for parents to educate themselves about their child's eligibility and the services that can be provided. Working closely with school psychologists or guidance counselors, teachers, special education personnel, or school administrators is critical in ensuring that the child receives the appropriate services. In some instances, it may be very helpful to talk with an educational consultant, educational advocate, or educational lawyer who has expertise in special educational plans and/or alternative school placements for youth with bipolar disorder.

Although it is crucial that an education plan be individualized to the needs of each child, some general accommodations that may be helpful for children with bipolar disorder include those used for other academic or emotional challenges.

- Reducing or eliminating homework demands. In some instances, it may also be possible to arrange for the child to work on homework during the school day.
- Access to a resource room for specific classes.
- Preferential seating in the classroom.
- A functional behavioral assessment and a behavioral program in the classroom.

- A program to increase communication between home and school (e.g., communication log).
- Specialized instruction for learning disabilities.
- Occupational or speech/language therapy.
- Maintaining a second set of textbooks at home.
- Reducing the number of classes taken or shortening the school day.
- A one-on-one or shared special education aide in the classroom.
- Allowing for extended time on tests.
- Reducing the need for handwriting assignments by using a keyboard or a scribe.
- A social skills group.
- In-school counseling.
- Identifying a point-person to whom the child can go and talk to if distressed or in crisis.
- Providing a quiet place where the child can calm down and relax.
- An extended school year (services over the summer).
- For children with more severe problems, placement in a separate therapeutic classroom within the school, alternative therapeutic day school, or residential program.

Planning Around College

It is important to know that, for children receiving special education services, services can be provided through the age of 21. Although there are differences between high schools and post-secondary programs in the services that they must provide, colleges will provide accommodations to enable the student with a disability to access the curriculum. In addition, many colleges offer more extensive supports for students with disabilities, and there are colleges and post-secondary programs around the country that have been specially designed for students with ADHD, learning disabilities, and/or emotional difficulties. More minor accommodations that may be helpful to students entering college include reducing the number of courses taken (in some instances, a college student with bipolar disorder may be considered a full-time student even with a reduced course load), maintaining as much structure as possible (e.g., seeking colleges with smaller class sizes or that mandate class attendance), and seeking designated quiet or "dry" dormitories (those that prohibit alcohol or drug use).

Helpful Parenting Strategies

Parenting a child with bipolar disorder can be a stressful and frustrating experience. First and foremost, it is important for parents to remember that they are not to blame for their child's difficult behaviors. It is also important to remember that these children are suffering from an illness that can get in the way of their behaving appropriately. Although their behavior in the moment can be quite outrageous, children often feel very remorseful or ashamed once the crisis has passed. In addition, the following general parenting strategies may be helpful.

- *Maintain structure and regularity in activities.* As with adults, children with bipolar disorder are vulnerable to disruptions in their schedules. They may benefit from a predictable schedule of activities that is not too hectic but avoids long periods of downtime. This can be particularly important during the weekends or vacation. Relaxing or soothing activities can also help a child during stressful periods or during particularly difficult times of day.
- *Keep a mood log.* A mood log or brief journal will help you identify patterns in your child's moods, identify potential triggers, and become aware of early warning signs of mood episodes.
- *Plan ahead.* As much as possible, avoid unnecessary situations that are likely to trigger meltdowns. If a difficult situation is unavoidable, prepare for it in advance (in collaboration with your child if they are old enough to do so).

- *Decrease family conflict.* It is important to decrease overall family conflict and stress because these can destabilize the moods of both children and adults with bipolar disorder. Pick and choose your battles carefully before imposing a limit. Be consistent in the limits you set, and enforce them in a firm but nonaggressive and nonconfrontational manner. If possible, involve your child in solving issues to teach him or her problem-solving skills. Remember that parents serve as models for child behavior, so, as much as possible, work to provide your child with frequent examples of step-by-step problem solving and conflict resolution (family therapy may help to a great degree here). If arguments become aggressive, implement strategies to de-escalate tension (e.g., a family time-out until all parties have calmed down). If parents disagree about how to handle a problem, avoid arguing or discussing this in front of your child.
- *Remember your child's strengths.* Encourage your child to channel their energies into appropriate tasks and activities. Remember to praise appropriate behaviors, and point out talents and positive traits.
- *Be aware of stressful events outside the home.* Stay in close contact with the school because stressors at school or with peers can lead to meltdowns at home. Talk with your child about these stressful events and ways of managing them.
- *Facilitate transitions.* Because transitions (including daily transitions) can be particularly difficult, provide plenty of warning for upcoming transitions (ranging from larger transitions such as school onset and offset and vacations to nightly bedtime) provide sufficient time for the child to transition at their speed, limit the number of unnecessary steps during transitions, and try to keep routines as consistent as possible.
- *Monitor your teenager's behavior.* Because teens with bipolar disorder are especially vulnerable to alcohol or drug abuse, as well as other risky behaviors, it is important that parents be aware of

their peer relationships and behaviors outside the home. Also keep close tabs on internet, instant messenger (IM), and cell phone use because impulsive behaviors can get your teen into trouble.

- *Have a crisis plan in place.* If your child can become violent or suicidal, develop an emergency plan ahead of time (be sure to include his or her treatment providers in this plan). Know which hospital you may want to use for an inpatient stay for your child, and know the steps needed for admission (see Chapter 8). At crisis times, make sure that dangerous items (e.g., knives and medications) are out of the reach of children. Maintain the safety of siblings and pets. Avoid confrontations in potentially dangerous situations (such as while driving in the car).
- *Be aware of unrealistic expectations.* It may be tempting to compare your child to other children (or his or her siblings). However, remember that just because you or others feel that a child should be able to do something does not mean that they can. Understand your child's special needs and work with them to achieve what they can at their own pace. Set intermediate goals that the child can work towards, step-by-step.
- *Take care of yourself.* Parenting a bipolar child or adolescent can be exhausting, stressful, and isolating. It is crucial that parents take time out for themselves to "recharge their batteries." Obtain support from family or others who understand what it is like to have a child with bipolar disorder. Consider additional resources in the community, including therapy, after-school programs, or support groups.

Transitioning to Adulthood

Adolescence to young adulthood can be a difficult period for those suffering from bipolar disorder. During this age range, young people must take increased responsibility for the life choices they make.

They will be expected to become increasingly independent (e.g., learning to drive, moving away from home, going to college), make appropriate choices, and manage challenges of everyday life. Likewise, this is a period during which self-esteem and self-confidence crystallize, and during which dreams and plans for the future take shape. It is also a period during which young people may be vulnerable to being derailed by poor choices or impulsive behaviors, and it is the time period during which bipolar disorder is most likely to emerge. That is, bipolar disorder can emerge at a time when a person is just getting ready to become more independent, have more a say in what they do and how they are going to do it, and take the next life steps (whether that be dating, college, a job, or moving out of parents' home). One effect is that young people with bipolar disorder must take on the challenge of managing a mood disorder—often with their parents' help—just when they want to break free of parental restrictions.

The good news is that the treatment strategies described in this book can be effective for adolescents and younger adults. In fact, there are indications that treatment might be especially effective the sooner it is started relative to the onset of bipolar disorder. However, this means that these young people must take on extra work—to manage moods, engage in structured problem solving and stress management, regularly take medication, and restrict recreational drug use—at a time when they are otherwise seeking to spread their wings and leap into adulthood. For example, a college student may need to take fewer courses in any given semester to reduce the level of stress and help protect against triggers for mood episodes. Although this may result in taking an extra year to compete college, it can help ensure a more successful and enjoyable college experience, without the severe disruptions in performance and goals that a mood episode may bring. Likewise, at most colleges there are numerous resources available to help students, including academic support, private tutors or life coaches, student mental health services, and support groups. Yet these resources typically must be actively sought out and requested. This shift in strategy can be hard for a young adult: to plan for restrictions and challenges exactly at a time of life when they are feeling invincible.

Medication Issues

Taking medication can be an especially difficult issue for adolescents and young adults. Some young people may feel that they are being "controlled" by medications, or may fear that the medication may take away their creativity, or represent an attempt by others to control them. Some young people, particularly if they have only had one or very few episodes, may be ambivalent about the diagnosis of bipolar disorder and may not believe that medications are necessary or helpful.

However, even for young adults and those with only one episode of mania, medication is an important part of treatment. In addition to decreasing the severity and frequency of mood episodes, medications can help improve the overall course of illness and increase the likelihood of returning to a productive, fulfilling life, if one has been derailed by mood episodes. Also, the first interactions and experiences that someone has with mental health professionals can have an impact on their attitudes towards treatment over time, and, as such, it is important that these be as positive and collaborative as possible. Time spent helping a young person understand that medications are being prescribed to help them further their personal goals, rather than restrict them, is especially important. Writing out the pros and cons of medication choices, and challenging unhelpful beliefs (e.g., medications are only for weird sick people, I don't want to be one of those people") should be a regular part of early discussions about medication. No one wants a diagnosis of bipolar disorder, but, rather than being stuck at a stage of denial, it is important to move forward and pursue what strategies offer the *best life while having bipolar disorder.*

Drugs and Alcohol

Although drugs and alcohol can become a problem at any point, young adults may be especially vulnerable to abusing substances. They may have a perception that these substances are harmless and fun, and that "everyone" their age may be using them, especially if they are spending time with other young people who are also drinking or using drugs. Unfortunately, there is accumulating evidence that early drug and alcohol use may not only worsen mood (for example, increase feelings of depression or mood instability), but may also be associated, among vulnerable individuals, with initial panic or psychotic symptoms. Binge drinking during early adolescence has also been linked with longer-term cognitive problems.

It is not uncommon for individuals to want to pursue a course of limited alcohol use ("I am not going to quit, but I will limit myself to only a couple of drinks"). We recommend that consideration of this option be pursued only after a full month of abstinence. Too often, the impairing effects of alcohol lead an intention of only one drink to slide into a lot of drinks. The first goal is to assess mood and functioning fully independent of alcohol, and, second, to find a level of alcohol use that is free of trouble. Any intention of limited drinking needs to be assessed relative to the reality of whether this strategy works. Among college students, social needs tend to be tied to drinking (e.g., alcohol as a way to break the ice at a party or give someone something to do). As such, students may need review of the range of ways to meet others and interact well at a party without using alcohol. In short, we want individuals to have the opportunity to find that *fun* at a party is not linked to alcohol use. We also would like to have them avoid learning *first hand* that level of alcohol use is strongly tied to poor grades in college, or that continued alcohol misuse worsens the course of bipolar disorder. Finally, most students need to be aware that level of alcohol use in college is less than what they imagine it to be. Those who drink tend to get more attention than those who do not.

When students are made aware of levels and the consequences of alcohol use, they are more likely to curtail their own drinking, if given additional skills to help them pursue goals other than drinking. In recent years, web sites have been better developed to communicate drinking risks and alternatives to college students. For example, at this writing, *www.collegedrinkingprevention.gov* provides a wealth of information and resources directed at preventing college alcohol overuse.

For the college student with bipolar disorder, the overall message about the cost of alcohol to life goals needs to receive much more emphasis. The essential parental message is that, regardless of what others are doing or whether recreational use of alcohol or drugs is or is not dangerous in general, for *your child* drugs and alcohol are a bad idea because bipolar disorder that makes this use more harmful. Fair or unfair, recreational drugs and alcohol are simply not options that mix well with bipolar disorder.

Problems with alcohol overuse may also emerge well before college age. Parents will need to give adolescents the message that, while they are devoted to their wellbeing and their need to pursue fun, alcohol and drugs are just not a good idea for them. Helping plan other ways to pursue fun and fit in socially may be particularly helpful in giving an adolescent a way to negotiate his or her social life without recreational drug use. Also, if parents are worried that their child may be having serious problems with alcohol or drugs, professional help is the answer. Substance use problems often start during adolescence and young adulthood, and can be missed because of a perception that it "is just a phase." Signs that your child may have such problems include having legal difficulties because of drug or alcohol use, using drugs or alcohol in situations that could be dangerous, using drugs or alcohol instead of doing other activities, or using drugs or alcohol in increasing amounts or over longer periods of time. It is easier to address problems that have recently begun than those that have been going on for some time. Take action.

Part II

Managing Your Disorder

7

Stress and Schedule Management

Role of Stress in Bipolar Disorder Episodes

Stress is hard on everyone, but in bipolar disorder, stress (such as interpersonal conflicts or financial setbacks) can make it more likely that mood episodes will occur. Sometimes even positive life events, such as getting married or starting a new job, can create enough stress so that mood episodes are more likely. Because of the influence of stress on bipolar disorder, those with the disorder will want to be especially skilled at ways to manage stess and its effects. This chapter presents strategies that can help you cope with stress.

Managing Your Sleeping Patterns

One impact that stressful events can have on you and your mood is through disruption of sleep. With stress, difficulties falling asleep become more common, but some individuals may also experience disrupted sleep in the middle of the night, or early morning awakening (with the inability to fall back asleep). Research has shown that changes in a normal sleep cycle increase the risk of episodes of

Maintaining regular sleep patterns can help stabilize your mood.

mania or depression. Because you cannot always avoid stress, maintaining regular sleep patterns can help stabilize your mood.

The first step in using sleep as a buffer against episodes of depression and mania is to wake up and go to bed at the same times, even on weekends.

Self-Guided Care: Sleep

Given what I know about my sleep habits, I recommend to myself that I get approximately _____ hours of sleep per night. To best keep my sleep cycle stable, I recommend a regular bedtime at _____ and a regular waking time at _____.

Although it may be tempting to stay up later and sleep in on weekends, this change in sleep may increase the chance of depression or mania. The bottom line is—the more consistent you are in maintaining a sleep schedule, the better your chances are of keeping your mood stable. This strategy does not have to be carried out in an all-or-nothing fashion. If you find it difficult to keep to a regular sleep schedule, you may simply choose to use a more defined schedule during stressful times.

If you are having difficulty sleeping, it may be helpful to pay attention to the following sleep tips.

- *Keep stress out of the bedroom.* Discussing your concerns about your life or family or doing work-like activities (e.g., paying bills and reading documents for work) should not take place in your bed or in the bedroom. Save the bedroom for bed activities. Worry or work at a desk, not in bed.
- *Use muscle relaxation techniques in bed.* Relaxation tapes may help you relax and feel even more comfortable in bed. Remember the goal is not to go to sleep but to become very comfortable in bed

so that sleep comes naturally. Commercially available relaxation tapes may help with this process.

- *Never compete to get to sleep.* If you find that you are having difficulty sleeping, do not try harder. Trying hard to get to sleep often has the opposite effect; it wakes a person up with feelings of frustration and anger. Instead, try to *enjoy being in bed and resting,* even if sleep does not come. Direct your attention to how comfortable you can be in bed (how the pillow feels or how good it feels to lie down and stretch), how relaxed your muscles feel, and how you can let your thoughts drift. In other words, let yourself be very passive about sleep. *Your job is to be comfortable in bed and let sleep come to you.*

- *Give yourself time to unwind before sleep.* Make sure the last hour of activity before bedtime is relatively passive. Do not pay bills, do not work out life problems, and do not review your workday, save these activities for earlier in the day when you are fresher. Before sleep, choose activities that are pleasant and take very little effort (e.g., television, reading, talking). Go to bed only after you have had a chance to unwind and feel more like sleeping.

- *Use a regular daytime cycle to help with nighttime sleep.* Avoid taking naps during the day. Use regular exercise (at least three hours before bedtime) to help increase sleep and induce normal fatigue. Reduce caffeine use (certainly eliminate caffeine use after noon), and be wary of drinking alcohol or smoking within several hours of bedtime. One way to establish a regular time for falling asleep is to have a regular time for waking up. Setting your alarm clock to a reasonable time and maintaining it throughout the week will eventually be helpful in stabilizing your sleep time.

- *Adjust sleep cycle before travel.* Traveling across time zones also has the potential to disrupt regular sleep patterns. Whenever possible, gradually adjust your sleep cycle over the course of several days to match that of the new time zone. However, if your travel will be brief, as in a business trip, it might be better to keep to your regular schedule and not switch to the new time zone.

Keeping a Regular Schedule

Changes in your mood have the potential to disrupt your schedule of daily activity. For example, when you are depressed, it may be difficult to get out of bed, and you may feel less motivated to pursue a busy schedule of activities. Alternatively when your mood is elevated, you may feel more energized and take on more activities or projects than usual. Structuring a regular pattern of activities and sticking to it can help stabilize your mood. By adopting a regular pattern of exercise, eating, work, and social interaction, you can provide external cues that help keep your biological clock on the correct time. You may think of yourself working with this technique much like a piano player uses a metronome to keep the correct rhythm. This pattern should include a balance of activities that are pleasurable and that lead to a sense of accomplishment.

In addition to acting as a buffer against stress, paying attention to your regular schedule of activities also may provide you with clues to the beginning of a mood episode. That is, when you notice that your patterns of activities are changing, it is a signal to you that a mood episode may be starting. This should serve as a reminder to speak with your doctor, therapist, or support system and to take measures to avoid a full-blown episode of mania or depression.

Keeping an activity chart can help you structure a personalized weekly pattern of activities that work for you. An activity chart also provides you with a way to help ensure that you stay involved in regular activities that you value. The first step in making an activity chart is to think about some of the enjoyable activities that you used to do or want to do. Once you identify these activities, write them in the box provided.

Activity Charting

An activity chart can be used to track and stabilize work and leisure activities. Using the chart provided, write in regular activities (such as your workday, regular appointments, and other commitments). Then, write in regular activities that you want to engage in during the week to provide some pleasant moments. For example, make sure that you become involved in exercise, a hobby, a favorite television show, or a movie on a Wednesday evening so that the entire week is less stressful. As you take time to ensure regular involvement in stress-buffering activities, please consider the list of potentially pleasurable activities provided here. The value of this list is that it encourages you to consider a range of regular activities that serve as pleasant events in your life as well as a buffer against stress. The aim is to help you achieve balance—to make sure your week contains a set of activities balanced for activity (exercise as well as rest), pleasure (work and play), and sociability (time with friends, time alone).

An activity chart can be used to track and stabilize work and leisure activities.

Self-Guided Care: Valued Activities

Exercise

_____

_____

_____

Social Activities

_____

_____

_____

Relationship Activities

_____

_____

_____

Movies, Theater, and Recreation

_____

_____

_____

Hobbies

_____

_____

_____

Work-Related Activities

_____

_____

_____

Exercise

Regular exercise (in the range of 3 times per week for a half hour each time) has been shown to work as an antidepressant for individuals with major depression, and can be a powerful force in helping people manage stress, anxiety and depressed mood. Accordingly, the activity list includes a variety of exercise-based activities that may offer you direct mood benefits.

When considering starting or changing your exercise routine, please plan an appropriate starting program relative to your level of fitness. Also, review your exercise plan with your physician so that you have her or his recommendations for the intensity of any new exercise regimen. In every case, it is important to start slowly and work up in intensity during weeks of exercise, rather than face the soreness and injury of an overenthusiastic start to a new exercise program. Also, it may be important to plan exercise activities with others, so that you have support in making regular exercise a priority for mood regulation.

Make sure your new pleasurable activities do not cut into your sleep time. Remember that a regular schedule can help you have more fun and less stress and at the same time help protect you from mood episodes.

Self-Guided Care: Activity for Mood Stabilization

The following list is designed to stimulate ideas for activities that may improve your weekly pleasure as well as provide stress-buffering effects. In considering the list, think of the *variations on themes* that may make an activity especially rewarding. For example, going swimming at a local pond instead of the local pool or grilling in a local park instead of your backyard may make your activity more memorable. Likewise, little things added to a regular activity—buying your favorite childhood candy at the movie theater or fixing a cup of hot chocolate to drink while reading a novel—transform an experience by evoking past pleasant memories.

Because the mood-promoting effects of exercise are powerful, the list begins with these activities. Any level of exercise is a good start, but over time, for exercise to have its desired effect on mood, you should exercise for 30 minutes a day, three days per week. When you go through the list, check off those activities of most interest to you.

- Take daily walks for pleasure
- Jog (park, track, gym)
- Rollerblade
- Ride a bicycle
- Go swimming
- Go windsurfing
- Try sailing
- Paddle a canoe or kayak
- Go fishing in a local stream or pond
- Go skiing
- Go ice skating
- Play tennis
- Kick around a soccer ball
- Join a softball league
- Play volleyball
- Shoot baskets with a friend
- Set up a racquetball date
- Call two friends and go bowling
- Play with a frisbee
- Take a kid to mini golf
- Start a program of weight lifting
- Take a yoga class
- Go to an indoor rock climbing center—take a lesson
- Build a snow fort and have a snowball fight
- Walk in the snow and listen to your footsteps
- Catch snowflakes in your mouth
- Sign up for a sculpting class
- Bake a cake

- Draw
- Paint (oils, acrylics, watercolor)
- Climb a tree
- Go for an evening drive
- Go to a drive-in movie
- See a movie
- Volunteer to work at a soup kitchen
- Join a museum Friday night event
- Write a letter to a friend
- Sing a song
- Play a musical instrument
- Take an art class
- Walk a dog
- Volunteer to walk dogs for a local animal shelter
- Play with children
- Visit a pet shop and look at the animals
- Sit in the sun
- Read in a rocking chair
- Sit on a porch swing
- Go for a hike
- Learn to knit
- Do a crossword puzzle (every day for a week)
- Go out for an ice cream sundae
- Rent a garden plot at a local farm or community space
- Grill dinner in the backyard
- Take a bath at night with candles around the tub
- Read the newspaper in a coffee shop
- Schedule a kissing-only date with your romantic partner
- Order hot chocolate in a restaurant
- Buy flowers for the house
- Get a massage

- Reread a book you read in high school or college
- Bake cookies for a neighbor
- Have a garage sale (perhaps with a neighbor)
- Wear purple
- Start a program of daily morning sit-ups or push-ups
- Get an atlas and look up a country you don't know about
- Buy a spool of wire and make a sculpture
- Go to an art museum and find one piece you really like
- Buy a magazine on a topic you know nothing about
- Polish all of your shoes
- Buy a new plant
- Clean out a closet
- Write a letter to the editor of the local newspaper
- Repaint a table or a shelf
- Go to a diner for breakfast
- Devote a meal to cooking red, white, and blue foods
- Plan an affordable three-day vacation
- Start a collection of heart-shaped rocks
- Find your top three favorite videos on YouTube and share them with a friend
- Woodworking—build a table or a chair
- Burn a CD of your favorite movie music
- Take a dance class
- Learn to fold dollar bills into origami creatures
- Soak your feet in warm water
- Learn to juggle
- Clean and polish the inside of your car
- Go to a concert
- Meditate
- Organize a weekly game of cribbage or bridge
- Look at a map

- Plan a drive in the country
- Sew some napkins
- Make a pizza and bake it
- Buy a cookbook and make three new meals
- Read a novel
- Listen to your favorite song from high school . . . really loudly
- Rent a video, make popcorn, and invite friends over

Social Time–Belonging to a Group

Regular social activities can be a powerful buffer against stress. Take some time to consider whether a regular group activity (on the order of once or twice a month) might provide you with a better sense of community and connection. Also, time with others is often time when you don't have to be self motivated. Plans with others may pull you away from time where you may be bored, inactive, or self-critical. Make good use of your social connections, and see how you might reach out to add more.

Schedule a Time for Solving Problems

To help keep worry out of your life, establish one or two specific times in your weekly schedule for dealing with life issues. Focusing on life issues as a regular part of the week helps ensure that life's problems do not become overwhelming. Having a regular time to focus on issues may also help prevent worrying on a daily basis. Worry, unlike problem solving, is not useful. It taxes your energy, time, and emotions. Worry is characterized by negative thoughts such as "It will be awful if _____ happens!" You may not even know whether it really will be awful if _____ happens, but the thought of something awful occurring is usually enough to increase your anxiety. If you usually spend a lot of time worrying, you will spend less time thinking about solutions.

Problem solving is a step-by-step approach to examine whether anything more effective can be done to make your life better. In order to make problem-solving strategies useful, we recommend that you devote at least one hour each week to evaluating your life issues using the following format. Go through this guided format carefully and slowly, writing as you go. It is designed to help you approach problem solving in a freer manner by separating the process of *coming up with options* from the process of *evaluating* and then *selecting* from these problem-solving options This method does not guarantee that you will come up with a good solution. It does, however, make sure that you think about the problem effectively and take the time to examine the best solutions you can think of on any given day. To help with you the problem-solving process, we have provided an example here.

Self-Guided Care: Problem Solving

What is the problem?

Arguments with my spouse about money

Why does this problem bother me (what are the specific features that bother me)?

I always end up being the "heavy"

I want a better sense of control over our finances

Is this a realistic problem (e.g., what do I really think is going to happen, and what part of this problem do I think is just worry)?

Yes, we really do argue quite often about money

How can I rewrite the problem clearly, so that it helps me think about a solution? Write in a clear restatement of the problem:

My spouse and I don't plan how to spend money, then are surprised by what each of us has spent, which leads to an argument

Now that I have the problem clearly in mind, what are potential solutions to this problem? To generate solutions, I want to think about as many possible solutions as I can (without thinking why they are good or bad, and without choosing an option at this point). What advice might a good friend give? If a friend had this problem, what advice would I give? Potential options:

1. *Don't do anything differently*

2. *Set up a weekly meeting with my spouse where we can discuss our finances and budgets*

3. *Open separate bank accounts*

4. *Use a notebook to track expenses and review with one another on a weekly basis*

5. *Assign a small amount of money as "free use" money and use a stricter budget for managing the rest*

Now rate each potential option. For each option rate the good and bad aspects of the proposed solution. Do not select an option until each is rated.

Good things about each solution   Bad things about each solution

1. *No effort required*   *Nothing is resolved and things may get worse*

2. *Give us a chance to talk openly about finances and make money issues more clear*

   I may end up hating the meetings and fighting with my spouse

3. *Gives each of us a sense of freedom*

   I would feel like we aren't partners and it would be really hard to divide the money

4. *Makes each of us accountable, makes sure we talk to each other about money, shows us where our money is going*

   We may fight during the meeting

5. *Like option 3, this gives us more freedom*

   The amount of "free use" money will likely change from month to month, and shouldn't we be buying things together?

Given this evaluation, which solution seems best?

Options 2 and 4 seem like the best solutions. Tracking our finances and meeting weekly seems to be a good way to start changing the situation.

Do you want to apply this solution, or is more time or more information needed to solve this problem?

Yes, I think we can start with this solution. I really want to change things and break the pattern of arguing over money.

Self-Guided Care: Problem Solving Schedule

My regular problem solving times will be:

_____(time) on _____ (day of the week) and/or

_____(time) on _____ (day of the week).

Self-Guided Care: Problem Solving

What is the problem?

_____

Why does this problem bother me (what are the specific features that bother me)?

_____

_____

_____

Is this a realistic problem (e.g., what do I really think is going to happen, and what part of this problem do I think is just worry)?

_____

How can I rewrite the problem clearly, so that it helps me think about a solution? Write in a clear restatement of the problem:

_____

_____

Now that I have the problem clearly in mind, what are potential solutions to this problem? To generate solutions, I want to think about as many possible solutions as possible (without thinking why they are good or bad, and without choosing an option at this point). What advice might a good friend give? If a friend had this problem, what advice would I give? Potential options:

_____

_____

_____

_____

_____

_____

Now rate each potential option. For each option rate the good and bad aspects of the proposed solution. Do not select an option until each is rated.

Good things about each solution   Bad things about each solution

1.

2.

3.

4.

5.

6.

Given this evaluation, which solution seems best?

_____

Do you want to apply this solution, or is more time or more information needed to solve this problem?

Positive Life Events

As joyful and wonderful as positive life events are, the exciting new relationships, school graduations, weddings, and job promotions can also substantially increase stress. In the management of bipolar disorder, it is important to plan well for the temporary surges in stress that go with positive events. Sometimes, to manage this stress, all it takes is the planning of extra moments of reflection to help you "catch up" emotionally to these events. Plan some time in your favorite chair with your favorite cup of tea or coffee (or your favorite person) to give time to feel the significance of these positive moments in life. These moments are deserving of extra reflection (echoing–see Chapter 14) to help them soak in pleasurably. Extra sleep or some good long walks or runs can also help translate these positive events into greater well-being, and can help buffer you against stress.

Avoiding Destructive Activities: Control over Substance Abuse

Drug and alcohol use represents a special risk for people with bipolar disorder. Using alcohol or drugs does not allow medications to work as well and causes people to forget to take them. It also is linked with a greater number of hospitalizations. In particular, stimulants (e.g., cocaine or speed) are known to trigger mood episodes in people with bipolar disorder, and using drugs like PCP, angel dust, or ketamine (special K) may trigger psychotic episodes.

Carefully consider whether you should drink alcohol, especially during periods when your mood is poor. Likewise, if alcohol is used in celebration, make sure it stays at a level that promotes wellbeing rather than problems. In considering use of alcohol, we want you to have your best interests in mind. Is your level of use of alcohol contributing to your life goals? And is it safe to use this alcohol given the presence of bipolar disorder? To give you a perspective on how you do when you are free of alcohol, we recommend every treatment plan start with a 30-day period of complete abstinence from alcohol and recreational drugs. This will provide you and your treatment providers a chance to evaluate the role these substances play in your life. Use other pleasant events (see previous list) to increase your enjoyment, and keep your treatment team aware of any substances that you use. Your doctor and therapist will provide additional strategies if necessary to help you manage substance use. Remember that you are a core member of your treatment team; make sure you keep the rest of your treatment team informed about triggers for your mood episodes.

> *If you have bipolar disorder, it pays to limit your drug and alcohol use.*

Table 7.1 *Activity Chart*

	Morning	*Midday*	*Afternoon*	*Evening*
Monday				
Tuesday				
Wednesday				
Thursday				
Friday				
Saturday				
Sunday				

Attention to Thinking Biases

Thinking Biases

Our thoughts can have a powerful effect on our mood, regardless of whether these thoughts are accurate or not. Also, ways of thinking become *automatic* over time, and unless you take a moment to "listen in" on what you are saying to yourself, you may be in a habit of coaching yourself very negatively. To help you get your goals met and to better care for your own mood, we would like you to become very adept at understanding and better at guiding your thoughts.

For this reason it is important to understand some of the common errors in thinking, and to develop thinking styles that serve rather than hurt your mood. A good starting point is to consider the role of "loaded words." These are words that communicate way too much emotion for the issue at hand. Loaded words include terms like "terrible," "horrible," "awful," or "disastrous." These terms are all descriptive of overwhelming negative emotional situations but otherwise convey little meaning. They also reduce efforts at coping and enhance self-blame. These words are also more likely to slip into use when you are in a bad mood. In this way, moods color your thinking patterns, and likewise, your thinking patterns can powerfully change your mood.

> *Thoughts don't have to be true to have powerful effects on emotion.*

For example, when you are depressed, you are more likely to think about a negative event in a more pessimistic way. This type of thinking can worsen a depressed mood, increase feelings of hopelessness, and decrease useful problem solving. This type of thinking is like looking at the world through darkly colored glasses that distort and darken reality in a negative way. The following are examples of thinking styles associated with depression that intensify negative thoughts and negative moods.

- Black or White Thinking. This type of thinking involves seeing events in terms of extreme categories. Things that happen are either *right or wrong, wonderful or awful, success or failure,* or *black or white,* without any gray or middle ground. This can also be referred to as all-or-nothing thinking.
- Personalization. This type of cognitive error involves seeing yourself as the cause of some negative event or situation without having any evidence to support this conclusion. For example, a friend cancels a lunch date and you assume that you must have done something to offend her.

During periods of depression, we would like you to be especially aware of negative and overly critical evaluations of yourself ("I blew it," "I am no good," "It never works out for me," "Look at me, I am . . . ") or of your future ("It won't work out," "there is no point"). During periods of depression, these thoughts tend to feel true (they are negative thoughts and they go with a negative mood state), but it is important to remember that thoughts in this form are extreme and do not do anything to guide you toward effective action.

Marveling refers to the process of appreciating the emotional tone of thoughts without buying into that emotion. In short, marveling is a "check this out; look at what I am saying to myself" attitude that helps people be aware of the tone of their thoughts without necessarily acting in response to these thoughts. Likewise, upon detecting a change in emotion, it is important to examine both the external situation ("What is going on?") and the internal environment ("What have I been saying to myself?"). Ideally, this process is completed with a sense of empathy toward oneself: "I am feeling bad; how can I understand what is going on, so that I can help myself?" This sort of self care is the direct opposite of tendencies toward self criticism when depressed. In fact, criticism of yourself around symptoms of depression ("look at me, I can't believe I am feeling down;" "I can't get out of bed, I am so defective;" "my concentration is off; I just can't do anything anymore") only serves to amplify this negative mood (creates a feed-forward cycle of depression about depression).

In considering the following sections, we would like you to keep in mind that your thoughts are useful only when they guide you effectively. If your thoughts are overly negative, overly positive, or overly critical, then they just can't have a role in helping you be more effective.

We would like you to get to know the thoughts in the following sections so that you can be ready to not take them too seriously and to be able to substitute more effective self-coaching when they occur. More effective coaching might include statements that not only acknowledge a problem but also suggest a course of action rather than global criticism (e.g., the thoughts, "Next time I need to approach this more carefully," "I should stop and plan," "I might need more practice to do this as effectively as I want," are all fair ways to coach yourself around a disappointment). Compare these thoughts with the motivation and esteem-sapping dysfunctional thoughts that follow.

- It is useless
- There is no point
- I will blow it anyway
- It will be just like last time when it did not go well

- I always fail
- I am no good
- I am different and flawed
- I should be different
- I should be better
- Look at me; I am not as good/happy/effective/bright/pretty as others

In being aware of negative thoughts, remember to notice the presence of *loaded words*. Words such as *failed* or *disaster* can make any situation or event seem more dire and depressing. We would like you to challenge such words ("what do I really mean by *disaster*; what about this situation really deserves that label?") so that you are reacting honestly to the situations at hand rather than overly emotional descriptions of the situation.

Hyperpositive Thinking

In contrast to depression, a hypomanic or manic mood brings with it feelings of overconfidence with your abilities, decisions, and ideas, and underestimations of the potential risks. New ideas may feel especially good, and friends and colleagues may seem too conservative or not open to good ideas or fun. Specific hyperpositive thoughts may include:

- This is a great idea; my thinking is better than ever!
- They (including my friends) are just trying to hold me back because they don't know how special I am.
- No one knows how to have fun anymore.
- People worry about rules too much; rules are for slow thinkers.
- I can do anything.
- My work is too important; I don't need sleep.
- I have never felt so sexy; I need to share myself with more partners.

These thoughts share the themes of overconfidence and the inability to accurately predict negative consequences. As a result, serious social, family, career, and financial complications may happen to you. Often these types of thinking patterns start gradually in a hypo-manic phase and escalate as mania develops. These types of changes in thinking should serve as a signal to you that your mood might be getting too high. Early action has the potential of reducing negative consequences.

Getting an Accurate Perspective on Thoughts

Remember that thoughts, whether true or not, can have a powerful effect on emotions. However, thoughts are only helpful if they are accurate. Mood disorders change the accuracy of thoughts: in depression they tend to be too negative and in mania they tend to be too positive.

To avoid being needlessly pushed around by inaccurate thoughts, it is important to treat thoughts as hypotheses, or guesses, about the world. Before accepting a thought

> *Thoughts are only helpful if they are accurate.*

as true, it is important to evaluate the thought to see whether it is truly helpful to you. Specifically, we encourage you to examine the evidence for and against a given thought and see if an alternative thought might offer a more accurate picture of reality. Remember that your thoughts will be influenced by your current mood. Don't let your moods push you into believing inaccurate thoughts.

If you have trouble sorting through your thoughts, it may be helpful to discuss your concerns with a trusted friend, family member, or therapist. In addition, the self-guided care box provided here may help you keep inaccurate thoughts from pushing your moods around.

Self-Guided Care: Evaluation of Thoughts

Is there an event that you find bothersome?

Event: _____

Write out the thoughts that occur to you about this event, and the moods that go with this thought.

(thoughts)   (moods)

_____   _____

_____   _____

_____   _____

_____   _____

What is the evidence for and against this thought? Does the thought just feel true, or is there actual evidence for this thought? Could this evidence support any other conclusions?

_____

_____

What evidence suggests this thought is true?

_____

_____

What evidence suggests this thought is false?

_____

_____

Are there alternative explanations of the event?

_____

_____

Given your evaluation of the evidence, is there a more accurate thought you want to substitute? _____

Suicidal Thinking and Self Care

At times, symptoms of bipolar disorder may include feelings of hopelessness. During intense times when symptoms are at their worst, things may *feel* so hopeless that life doesn't seem worth living. These feelings might also include thoughts of wanting to harm oneself or commit suicide. Suicidal thoughts can be overwhelming and frightening in their own right and may occur during both the depressive and manic phases of the disorder.

The most important thing to remember about suicidal thoughts and behaviors are that they are *symptoms of your illness* and just like other symptoms of bipolar disorder, they can be treated. With

> *Suicidal thoughts and behaviors are symptoms of your illness and they can be treated.*

help, the majority of people with bipolar disorder do feel better. A first step to managing the risk of suicide in bipolar illness is for both individuals with bipolar disorder and their families to be familiar with the warning signs of suicide. Some of these include:

- Talking about suicide or frequent talking or thinking about death
- Making comments about being hopeless, helpless, or worthless

- Saying things such as "It would be better if I wasn't here" or "I want out"
- Worsening depression
- Sudden changes in mood (e.g., being very sad to very calm)
- Voluntarily putting oneself in harm's way
- Putting affairs in order (e.g., organizing finances or giving away possessions to prepare for one's death)

If these warning signs emerge, we want you to take steps to protect yourself and your family by discussing these symptoms with your clinician. Again, suicidal thoughts are symptoms and they need to be reported to a qualified mental health professional so that you can get help. Depending on the severity of these thoughts, this help may include a brief hospital stay. Remember that the purpose of this stay is to protect you until you feel better. This is the most basic and crucial aspect of care—a person needs to be protected during periods of severe symptoms so that he or she has the chance to improve. We want you to take every step to provide this protection and to use your treatment team in this process.

Avoiding a Permanent Solution to a Temporary Problem

One straightforward strategy that has been shown in research studies to enhance safety in situations where an individual may be at risk for self harm is to make the process of getting help *easy*. The simple step of having all relevant contact information handy has itself been shown to protect individuals from suicidal actions. We want you to create contact numbers and information on an index card, and then share this card with those who care about you. Store this card in an easy to find place (e.g., a drawer, inside a kitchen cabinet, in front of your personal phone book). On this card, record the names and phone numbers of your treatment providers as well as phone numbers for the local emergency room and the phone number for the admissions personnel for the hospital *where you would prefer to get help.* Another important strategy for minimizing the risk that you will harm yourself is to include a suicide prevention plan as part of your Treatment Contract (see Chapter 13). You can work with your clinician and support team to incorporate this important planning component into your treatment contract so that everyone involved learns the warning signs to watch for and actions to take if you feel that you are slipping into suicidal thoughts.

In addition to a plan, both the individual with bipolar disorder and his or her family should know what to do in case of an emergency.

- Call your clinician or make arrangements for emergency care right away if you feel suicidal
- Ask for help from friends or family members to stay safe until you can get help

Call 911 or other emergency services if you:

- Think you cannot stop from harming yourself
- Hear voices
- Want to commit suicide

In all cases, it is important to protect yourself until you are in a position to recover and feel better.

Treating Yourself Well

In summary, thoughts do not need to be true to have powerful effects on your emotions. Because of this, we would like you to develop more accurate thinking patterns, especially when you are in a mood episode. This attention to your thinking style should also include attention to the tone of your self talk. You may even spontaneously note that as you work to better *marvel* at the content of some of your thoughts, you may find yourself developing a kinder attitude toward yourself. This is what a good friend or good therapist provides for you, and this is what we want you to provide to yourself–an open, accepting, and caring attitude that is designed to help you in general, and to help you specifically in the better management of mood episodes. Anyone who has to struggle with the mood episodes of bipolar disorder deserves kindness–especially from themselves. Talk to yourself in a reasonable tone using reasonable words.

Relationships and Communication Skills

Sharing This Chapter

This chapter has two goals. The first is to provide you with information about communication strategies. The second is to provide this information to your family members or friends who are living with you. Sharing this chapter with your family is important because bipolar disorder can be a stressor on the whole family and household stress (including conflicts between people) can influence the number of episodes of depression or mania that you experience. In short, it is beneficial to you and your family to improve communication skills at home, to minimize stress, and, hopefully, to reduce the likelihood of future mood episodes.

How Can My Family or Support System Help?

Your family or support system can play a crucial role in helping you cope with bipolar disorder. They can help put into action coping plans when you are high and help boost your mood and provide helpful activities or support when you are low (see Chapter 13). They also provide you with the joy and wellbeing that is so needed when your mood is stable. We encourage you and your support system to read this book in its entirety. It is particularly important for you to review the content of this chapter with your family or other support network.

Think of your family or other support network as part of your treatment team. You will need to decide with them how they can assist with your care. Make sure your support team understands the importance of your psychiatric care. You may want to review Chapter 3 with them to ensure that they understand the importance of your medication treatment. Likewise, reviewing the following sections may be especially important for improving communication between you and your family or support team.

Improving communication is one way to reduce stress at home and improve family relations. A tolerant and low-key atmosphere at home may be particularly important for reducing episodes of depression or mania. Of course, maintaining a low-key atmosphere can be very difficult at times. Patients and families often face a dilemma when confronting emotionally charged issues. Patients frequently complain that every strong emotion they have is attributed to bipolar disorder, while family members complain that the person is too reactive to emotional issues. Also, it may cause frustration when a member of your support system tries to avoid topics of discussion that he or she thinks are too intense for you. A helpful technique in this circumstance is the whisper rule. This requires a simple agreement that when anyone feels like a topic is getting hot, they can request the discussion be held in a whisper. If the rule is violated, the conversation is put off for a set period of time (e.g., two hours). Patients who use this technique often instruct their families to take their ability to follow the whisper rule as a sign that their mood state is normal and to consider times when they are unable to follow this rule as an indication of being ill.

> *Improving communication can reduce stress at home and improve family relationships.*

Communication Skills

For discussions between family members or members of a support network, it is useful to keep in mind a gardener's tip:

"It pays to water the flowers, not the weeds."

This tip underscores the importance of paying attention to what is working in your relationships, not what is going wrong. To water the flowers in your relationships you need to make sure that your family members know when they have done something that pleases you (e.g., being considerate, helping at home, etc.). All too often, individuals focus on and express only negative feedback. They complain about what isn't working, and this negative attention may increase bad feelings and fail to solve problems.

Attending to solutions rather than problems is especially important when a family member has a mood disorder such as bipolar disorder. Problems must be solved, but criticism and other forms of negative feedback may do more to worsen negative moods than to help with the issues at hand. Instead, more effective forms of communication need to be adopted.

Family members often have the greatest power when they are approving of others. Use this power! Make sure that you let others know when they are on track. This includes giving verbal feedback ("You know, I really liked it when you . . ."), using a positive tone, making pleasant eye contact, and giving touches or hugs when others are doing things you appreciate. These are important strategies for use by individuals with bipolar disorder, and they are also crucial strategies for helping reduce negative emotions in the family.

Effective Listening

All too frequently, arguments and bad feelings arise in relationships because of misunderstandings about what was being said. Each party jumps to conclusions, emotions escalate, and feelings of anger, frustration, or hopelessness may result. To avoid this scenario as much as possible, it is important to ensure that communication is clear. A message must be received before a second message is sent.

Effective listening refers to the skill of making sure that you accurately hear the speaker's message and accurately communicate to the speaker that you heard it. To be an effective listener it is important to try to understand what the speaker is actually saying. To do this, you need to keep your reactions or counter-arguments under control long enough to devote attention to the message. Your job is not to have a quick answer, but to show the person speaking that you have heard her or his message. Once a clear message has been received, then and only then should you consider reacting to the message.

> *To be an effective listener it is important to try to understand what the speaker is actually saying.*

The following outline includes the core steps of effective listening. Under the best of conditions, both you and your partner in conversations will agree to use these effective listening strategies. These strategies may slow down a conversation, but in turn may greatly reduce time that may have been spent in a hurtful argument.

- Give the speaker clear signs that you are attending to what he or she is saying. Look at him or her in the eyes and nod as you hear each point.
- Ask questions to clarify individual points. Your goal is not to debate an issue, but to understand the speaker's perspective.
- Verify that you have heard the speaker's issues correctly by repeating the core content to the speaker. If the speaker does not agree, do not debate what was said (e.g., "but you said . . ."); instead, devote attention to getting the message clear.
- Once the speaker and you agree on the message, then it is your turn to respond. When you respond, the goal is to explain your perspective while respecting your listener's perspective.

If you are on track with these effective listening skills, you may notice having a very different experience in your mind during communications with your partner. Instead of waiting to find ways in which your partner is wrong or incorrect (or defend against the perception that you are wrong or incorrect), you will find yourself instead feeling more relaxed and more curious about what your partner has to say. You will be less likely to enter into a debate, and more likely to have a sense of marveling at how your partner's experience is different from yours.

By way of example, when looking at the evening sky, rather than arguing whether the sky is more red, or pink, or blue as the sun sets, your job is to understand what colors are most apparent to your partner. Only by first understanding what your partner is seeing and emphasizing in her or his account of the sky can you have a full discussion. To facilitate this process, couples' therapists sometimes have a couple in conflict imagine that there is a large basket in the room between the couple. When one partner speaks, the listener is to imagine the information going into the basket. The job of the listener is to examine the information and try to understand it. The reason for the basket image is so that the listener does not get the communication *on them*, and have to push the communication away. Instead, the listener is to try to intently understand the perspectives (not facts to be debated) of the speaker. The goal is to understand this information first, communicate it back to the speaker second, and then explain your own perspective, third. And when it is your turn to provide information, it will be important to do it in a way that is easy to *pick up* from the basket. As illustrated in the Self-Guided Care box, starting your message with an accusation ("You always. . .") will encourage defensiveness and counter-attack ("Yeah, well you always. . .") By instead sticking to your concerns and feelings ("I feel sad when. . . .") more useful communication can result. This step-by-step approach can help reduce conflict, and reducing conflict in communications is helpful for the management of bipolar disorder.

Self-Guided Care: Using Better Communication

To help you get what you want, it is important that you use language that is useful for your goals. Practice restating negative statements in ways in which you are more likely to get your partner's attention and action.

When you feel like saying:

"*I am sick of this! You always* _____!"

Instead you could say (be specific and offer solutions):

"I feel really upset when you _____. It really would be helpful if you could instead _____."

Requesting Changes in Behavior

Remember that your goal with requests is to achieve a change in behavior. Your job is not to punish or shame. Punishment and shame often intensify the negative emotions in the household, further sapping joy from everyone's interactions. If you are going to request a change, you want to do it in a way that gives your listener a chance to succeed.

Instead of using a critical statement (e.g., "You never help me with anything around the house"), use a positive request for change that directs your partner toward success (e.g., "It would mean a lot to me if you could help me with some of the chores around the house"). Rather than act like an authority, do your best to enlist the listener's problem solving efforts. For example, you may ask for help with chores around the house and then suggest that your partner join you in listing and dividing up some of the chores.

Finally, when negative feelings are expressed, it is important to express these feelings in a specific rather than a general way. Avoid terms such as "you always . . ." or "you never. . . ." These terms often serve to push away the listener, decreasing the chance you will get what you want. Instead, approach your partner (or other listener) with respect, describe what is upsetting you in specific terms, and make specific recommendations about how your partner can help things go better next time.

None of these skills guarantee that any given discussion will not deteriorate into a frustrating argument. However, use of these skills should help decrease the amount of conflict and bad feelings in your relationships over time. It takes practice to use these skills well.

Communicating With Your Clinician

Communication problems can frequently arise between patients and their clinicians. Patients and doctors are frustrated when the time allotted for a scheduled appointment runs out and important issues are not addressed. Your clinician needs to record information about your symptoms and response to treatment at every visit. Increasing the quality and the amount of information you provide at each visit also improves the quality of care you receive. You can accomplish this in a time-efficient manner by using a daily mood chart to effectively communicate your level of symptoms. One such mood chart is provided in Chapter 12; take a look at this chapter, discuss with your clinician, and see whether this mood chart can be used to summarize information on symptoms for your sessions with your clinician. With symptom information nicely summarized on the mood chart, more time is available to spend on other topics of importance to you.

Talking About Problems with Your Clinician

In the treatment of bipolar disorder, patients and their families may face frustration with medications, side effects, difficulties scheduling, and hurt feelings as they work with care providers. It is important to not let these frustrations get in the way of getting needed care. Stay vigilant of whether you are getting your needs met by your care, and whether you get into any bad habits of avoiding appointments (making them more slowly or missing or cancelling existing appointments) due to conflicts with your provider. We encourage you to discuss conflicts and goals early and often with your care providers, using some of the same communications skills discussed above. We want you to establish and keep a close link with your care providers so that you can best work with them to get your care goals met. If regular problems in communication arise that cannot be solved, talk with your provider about getting a consultation or a consultation leading to a referral so that your treatment stays on track.

Managing Irritability and Anger

Feelings of irritability and anger are fundamental symptoms of bipolar disorder that can occur as part of hypomanic, manic, or depressive episodes. When anger and irritability emerge as part of (hypo)mania, they often occur with a sense of internal pressure, including a humming sense of urgency, burden, or sensitivity to comments or actions from others. At times, individuals with bipolar disorder describe these feelings as a need to look for a fight, almost like they are seeking an explanation for the emotional tone in their bodies ("Oh yeah, I knew there was a reason I was feeling angry, it is because he/she is . . ."). When you experience this type of irritable mood, you focus your attention on potential slights and errors. Once you notice a small infraction, all of the irritable emotion is set into play ("I am so sick of this, I am going to put a stop to this right now") and an unnecessary argument or a self-defeating outburst can result.

Irritability and anger also emerge as part of depressive episodes. For many individuals, depressive irritability is similar to the feeling of having a constant toothache; because of the constant backdrop of pain, there is the sense of not being able to cope with much more. Sounds seem louder and shrill, imperfect behavior from others feels more intolerable, problems seem more catastrophic, and requests from others feel more overwhelming. At times, urges to fight against these annoyances are intensified by an internal sense of agitation, an inability to sit still, where the next annoyance feels like the perfect target to communicate, "stop it, stop it, stop it!" Similar to the feelings in irritable hypomania, the angry outburst feels justified at the moment. But later, when a sense of perspective returns, the thought is frequently, "I can't believe I got so upset and acted that way."

Part of effectively coping with bipolar disorder involves becoming skilled with understanding and reducing the impact of irritability and anger. One strategy for coping with irritability is to consult with your psychiatric provider to see if a medication adjustment may help keep these emotions in check. It is also useful to see how well you can develop additional anger management skills to break the links between mood disturbances, irritability, and aggressive behavior. In preparing to consider these skills, it is important to remember that the goal of anger management is to maximize your own wellbeing. Efforts to control anger do not deny the annoyances or frustrations in life. Instead, efforts to control anger are directed at avoiding the additional mood problems and strained relationships that anger causes.

Good anger management skills can break the links between mood disturbance, irritability, and aggressive behavior.

To achieve your goals of reducing anger and irritation, we suggest rehearsal of four related skills. These skills are aimed at reducing the emergence as well as the escalation of anger. Should these preventive efforts fail, they are also targeted at minimizing aggressive behavior once it is initiated. Together, these four principles are designed to help you reduce the cost of irritability and anger episodes to your mood and to your relationships and work goals:

1. Don't let poor thinking habits goad you into an angry outburst or argument.
2. You don't have to solve an irritation *right now.*

3. Beware of win/lose thinking.

4. Remember to selfishly value your life goals, even when angry.

The remaining sections provide information on putting these principles to use.

Poor Thinking Habits and Anger

Keep your thoughts from pushing you around. Especially when feeling irritated, we would like you to be able to quickly evaluate and defuse thoughts that may help magnify annoyances into anger. These magnifying thoughts are of two primary types. One type serves to bring past annoyances and frustrations forward into the present so that any minor annoyance is weighted with these old emotions. The result is that a minor annoyance gets linked with a long cascade of irritating patterns that *must be stopped now.* For the examples that follow, notice how these thoughts can amplify a minor irritation into a major issue. We want you to get to know these thoughts so that they can't ignite irritation into a major anger episode.

- This is just like last time
- I can't let her/him/them get away with this
- They are always doing this to me
- Enough is enough
- I can't let this happen again
- I am always being treated this way
- They always act this way

These thoughts act to make the issue at hand too important and make you feel like you need to take a stand *right now.* Intensity of emotion is increased in part by taking past frustrations and bringing them forward to the present moment. In effect, these thoughts work to goad you on toward a more explosive conflict.

A second way to intensify anger and lose perspective is to guess at the motives of others. By using the right kind of self-talk, you can make an annoyance seem more like a personal attack. Take a look at the thoughts that follow and notice the way in which they increase a sense of victimization and anger.

- They are messing with me
- I am sick and tired of being manipulated
- They don't respect me
- She/he is out to get me
- He/she is doing this on purpose
- He does not care how I feel
- She knows I hate this and is getting even
- If I don't correct her/him now, this will go on forever

Again, the purpose of getting to know these thoughts is to become successful at coaching yourself more effectively through conflicts so that you can better reduce the impact of anger and irritability on your relationships and personal goals.

You Don't Have to Solve This Issue Right Now

Anger can amplify the perceived importance of an issue to the neglect of other important life considerations. It feels important, it has the full pressure of irritable mood behind it, but it is crucial to remember—you don't need to solve the issue now. No matter how important the issue feels it is always important to give yourself time to cool down and consider other strategies to solve the issue at hand.

It is always important to give yourself time to cool down and consider other strategies to solve the issue at hand.

For example, to get out of a conflict quickly and buy time to think things through, you might say:

This really upsets me. Let me think about this problem, and then we can talk about it more at a later time. I want to work out a better way of dealing with this.

The goal is keep others (e.g., your friends, family, coworkers) engaged in wanting to work things out with you. Buy yourself time to see how much extra irritation might be due to a mood episode rather than a result of the conflict at hand. You can always come back to this problem later. There is no reason to act like the present is the crucial moment for solving this issue. Remember, you always have time to devote to anger in the future if you choose, but *you only have right now to prevent a current angry outburst.*

Also, once it becomes clear to you that you are in a period of irritability, you will want to think about what events or meetings you might like to cancel. Some individuals choose to take a sick day at times of increased irritability. By staying home, or rescheduling the most crucial family events or work meetings, you can reduce the likelihood that these events will go badly. In short, invest in your future by making sure that brief periods of irritability do not have a long-term effect by reducing the opportunities for damaging arguments.

Beware of Win/Lose Thinking

Thinking about having to win an argument can prevent you from making more useful choices in a time of irritability and anger. Irritability itself fuels a sense of needing a *win now.* Even when you know intellectually that stopping an argument might be the best option, your irritability may keep you in the mood to prolong the conflict. Don't do it! When feeling irritable, we would like you to remember the following:

You don't have to win this argument; instead you need to maximize how well your life is going.

Sometimes, the best way to truly *finish* an argument well is to save yourself the *guilt and regret* that come from an overblown conflict. When you cool down, you may realize that there were other alternatives for handling the conflict that would not have led to so many hurt feelings, disrupted friendships, or professional challenges. In helping yourself get out of an argument gracefully, keep in mind the following thoughts that may keep you locked into an argument in a way that does not serve you well.

- I can't let her/him win
- I can't let them get away with this
- I can't lose
- I know I have a point somewhere in here; I am going to force him/her to get it

Remember to Value your Life Goals, Even When Angry

Anger and irritability increase the sense of *I need*. We want you to be able to key into this feeling when you are irritable and angry, but then to use this feeling to guide you toward effective and calm action. For example, when angry, you might think the following:

> *I am frustrated. I can feel my irritability humming along, and I can feel the urge to pick a fight. But I know how it feels after the argument, or a few days later when my mood is different. Even though I have the urge to pick a fight, what would serve me better than having extra conflict?*

The crucial question we want you to ask yourself is the last one, "What can I do now that would *serve me* better than having a conflict?"

In trying to find an answer to this question, don't forget to enlist the help of those who care about you. You don't always have to deal with anger or irritability on your own; find a way to defuse an argumentative evening before it starts. Two examples are provided here that illustrate ways in which you may want to notify a loved one that you are more on edge, and to ask for help in having a better evening either with your loved one (example 1) or on your own (example 2).

> *I am really having a bad day with lots of frustration and irritability. I would love to sit down and talk about ways we can make the evening go well. I may not be in a very good mood, but I bet we can work together to make the evening go better than it might otherwise go.*

> *I am really having a bad day with lots of frustration and irritability. This might be a good evening for me to find a way to entertain myself alone, because I don't want my irritability to affect the family or you. How can we plan the evening so that we both get some nice break time?*

In summary, irritability and anger occur frequently with the mood episodes of bipolar disorder. We want you to be ready for these emotions and the thoughts that go along with them. By being ready for the thoughts that intensify anger and keep you engaged in arguments, we hope you will become better at defusing these patterns. Particularly when you are feeling irritable, we want you to treat yourself well. Chapter 7, focusing on planning pleasant events, may serve you well at these times.

Focusing on Life Goals

By its nature, bipolar disorder disrupts life goals and daily plans. Although episodes of mania are responsible for dramatic disruptions—the hospitalization that interfered with the completion of a semester of school, the financial crisis that dominated the marital agenda, or the angry outbursts that led to a job dismissal—depressed moods lead to more longstanding interference with the motivations, goals, relationships, and work habits of individuals with bipolar disorder and their families. Depending on the length and severity of these mood episodes, job functioning may be interrupted, relationships may be strained, friendships may lapse, and educational or social plans may be put off. Accordingly, during periods of stability, individuals with bipolar disorder may have a sense of needing to *catch up* with life agendas that have been disrupted.

We Want to Caution against This Strategy

If we would try to identify one overarching principle to keep in mind relative to the life disruptions of bipolar disorder it is, you don't *get behind* in life; you *experience* life. Life events can always take a linear, planned life and make it more unexpected, more curvilinear, more like the zigzagged course toward goals depicted in Figure 11.1. Mood episodes

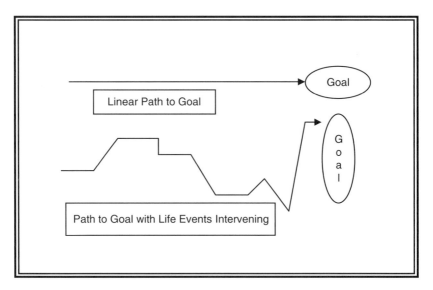

Figure 11.1 *Paths to Life Goals.*

are such events, and as those with the disorder know well, bipolar brings about multiple mood episodes.

Rather than being useful, the strategy of trying to make up for lost time increases stress, guilt, and anxiety, and exaggerates the importance of every interaction and event. In other words, trying too hard to *catch up* in life is a way to increase some of the very mood problems that led to life disruptions in the first place.

But What Is the Alternative?

We recommend two primary strategies. First, we want you to be vigilant to the overly critical and self-defeating thinking patterns that were reviewed in Chapter 8. Be mindful of these patterns especially relative to how you talk to yourself about those life goal that become *markers* of your success. In particular we want you to avoid "I should have . . ." statements like, "I should have a better [house, car, lover, job, retirement fund, etc.]." These *should* statements tend to direct attention away from some of the pleasures and meaning in life—wanting to achieve something in life, wanting a human connection, and wanting to have some fun along the way—and over-focus attention on specific markers that are only indirectly linked to these larger goals. Joy often lies along the path of achieving goals, rather at the endpoint. Which means all those statements that "life would be different if only I had. . ." are probably not as true as they feel. The goal is to focus your attention on where you go next, rather than on where you should be. Using arbitrary markers of *should* leads to a sense of being behind, and worse, a sense of having to catch up.

As a second strategy, we want you to acknowledge that bipolar disorder may change the pacing by which you go after life goals. In short, we encourage you to plan your life goals in relation to strategies that most reduce the likelihood of a new episode. All of the previous chapters include attention to this goal. For example, stress management, problem-solving skills, communication skills, and helping you think about medications as tools are all designed to help minimize the impact of bipolar disorder on your life. In the same way, we want you to think about honing your attention to the step-by-step movement toward the goals that you think are most important.

Choosing Goals Instead of Markers of Goals

If your bipolar disorder has disrupted your progress toward your life goals—such as progress through college, the quality of your relationships, or your job attainment—we would like you to be especially careful of using a specific marker as evidence that you are "back on track." That is, before accepting a life goal, we would like you to play the *Why Game.* The Why Game is a strategy to help people clarify

Goal as a (False) Marker	Goal for Joy and Security
I need to buy my own house.	I need to buy my own house.
Why?	*Why?*
It would make me happy.	It would make me happy.
Why?	*Why?*
Because it is important for adults to have their own house.	Because I want to spend money on something I own and take care of.
Why?	*Why?*
Because it is a marker of responsibility.	Because I think home prices are going to appreciate, and if I can get into a home it will be a great investment. I don't like giving that money over for rent.
Why?	*Why is this important?*
Because only losers continue to rent.	It is part of a plan for my future financial security.
Why is this important?	*Why else is it important?*
I want others to think well of me. I want to prove that I am on track.	I want to be able to decorate my own place and take care of my home. I think it will make me happy.
Why is this important?	
Uh, I think I am trying to manage perceptions, rather than trying to find happiness for myself.	

goals, and to make sure goals are being pursued for a good reason. For example, the Why Game around buying a house may lead to two very different motivations.

After you clarify your goals, the worksheets provided allow you to consider the goals you think are particularly important for the coming year. In thinking through these goals, consider the social, relationship, financial, educational, work, and family domains.

The starting point for considering these goals is important. Please do not start with the goals you want *if your life unfolds ideally.* Instead, attend to *where you are now,* and attend to the several life goals that would make you feel that you are progressing in the direction that you want. In particular, we want you to use the phrase, "Given where I am now, I would like to devote effort to _____." The worksheets that follow are designed to help you with this process.

Self-Guided Care: Achieving Goals Using Pacing

The purpose of this form is to help you think through your long-term goals and to formulate a step-by-step plan for achieving them. In addition to helping you identify and arrange the intermediate steps necessary for achieving larger goals, this worksheet is designed to remind you that achieving your goals is a process that unfolds slowly over time.

Please identify for this year, a few goals that seem important to you. Please list these goals and then consider and write down why the goals seem important. You may also want to discuss some of these goals with family or friends.

Goal 1:_____

Why does this matter to you (watch out for *should* statements)?

_____

_____

_____

Goal 2: _____

Why does this matter to you (watch out for *should* statements)?

_____

_____

_____

Goal 3: _____

Why does this matter to you (watch out for *should* statements)?

_____

_____

_____

Now that you have identified your goals, please use the next worksheet to plan the intermediate steps that are important for ensuring that you are on track for achieving your larger goals. Please use a separate sheet for each of your larger goals.

Steps to Goal Attainment

Long-term goal:

_____

_____

_____

Short-term goal:

Short-term goal:

Short-term goal:

Short-term goal:

NOW Your current situation:

_____

_____

_____

12

Mood Charting

Why Is Mood Charting Important?

Mood charting is recommended because it enables you to detect early signs of changes in your mood and communicate this information to your care providers. Mood charting can also help you and your treatment team to intervene early to prevent severe episodes.

An advantage of mood charting is that you become more familiar with the patterning of your mood and your personal triggers for mood changes. For this reason, there is a place on your mood chart to note your daily stressors. There is also space to track your medication doses. Also, disruptions in sleep have the potential for triggering episodes; the mood chart also will help you to watch out for early changes or disruptions in your sleep cycle and to intervene early in collaboration with your clinician.

> *Mood charting can help you detect early signs of changes in your mood.*

The mood chart not only has immediate value in summarizing your mood and stressors for your clinician, but it also has value as a record over time. The longer you keep a consistent mood record, the more you can potentially discover about the natural patterns and triggers for your mood episodes. As such, think of the completion of the daily mood chart as an investment in your future. By making mood charting a regular part of your routine, you and your clinician will have a wealth of information in the future for understanding your pattern of mood changes, and this pattern may aid in your future treatment planning.

> *The mood chart can take as little as 20–30 seconds a day to complete.*

Completing Your Mood Chart

At first glance, the mood chart can appear complicated. This is a very common reaction. However, the mood chart can take as little as 20–30 seconds a day to complete. The directions that follow will help you to fill out your mood chart.

At the start of the day

- Simply record the number of hours of sleep you got last night.

At the end of the day

- Rate your mood, making two ratings—the highest and lowest your mood reached during the day. If your mood did not fluctuate, these two ratings may be one and the same. The abbreviation WNL stands for *within normal limits* and refers to a stable or normal mood state.
- Rate your anxiety: None = 0; Mild = 1; Moderate = 2; Severe = 3.
- Rate your irritability: None = 0; Mild = 1; Moderate = 2; Severe = 3.
- Make notes about any stressful or positive events that occurred during the day.

- Record the number of tablets of each medication actually taken.

On a monthly basis

- Record your weight.
- For women, circle the dates when menstruating.

Bring the Mood Chart to Every Clinical Visit

As part of creating a collaborative working relationship with your clinician, we recommend establishing a policy of making the review of the mood chart a part of every session. By showing your clinician your mood chart at the start of each session, you will have more time to focus on issues of importance to you. Most importantly, the mood chart will enable you and your treatment team to maximize the likelihood of good treatment outcomes by keeping close track of symptom patterns over time. The mood chart gives you another tool for maintaining awareness and control over the course of your disorder.

Being a Good Scientist About Your Mood

Over time, your mood chart can provide you with a valuable record of how your moods and mood swings seem to work. Looking back over old mood charts may help you see how stress or low sleep helps set off a mood episode. You may also notice ways in which mood highs precede mood lows, and this information can help you work toward better management of your mood. If you notice patterns like these in your mood, discuss them with your treatment team. The goal is to generate new ideas about how to keep your mood in the range you want.

								Daily Notes
Name_____								Mood Chart Month/Year

TREATMENTS
(Enter number of tablets taken each day only)

___ mg	___ mg	Antipsychotic ___ mg	Antidepressant ___ mg	Anticonvulsant ___ mg	Benzodiazepine ___ mg	Lithium ___ mg	Psychotherapy	Daily Notes
								Weight

Figure 12.1 *Mood Chart.*

MOOD
Rate with 2 marks each day to indicate best and worst

			Depressed			WNL		Elevated			

Irritability	Anxiety	Hours Slept Last Night	Severe — Significant Impairment NOT ABLE TO WORK	Mod. — Significant Impairment ABLE TO WORK	Mild — Without significant Impairment	MOOD NOT DEFINITELY ELEVATED OR DEPRESSED NO SYMPTOMS Circle date to indicate Menses	Mild — Without significant Impairment	Mod. — Significant Impairment ABLE TO WORK	Severe — Significant Impairment NOT ABLE TO WORK	Psychotic Symptoms Strange Ideas, Hallucinations
						1				
						2				
						3				
						4				
						5				
						6				
						7				
						8				
						9				
						10				
						11				
						12				
						13				
						14				
						15				
						16				
						17				
						18				
						19				
						20				
						21				
						22				
						23				
						24				
						25				
						26				
						27				
						28				
						29				
						30				
						31				

Key: 0 = none, 1 = mild, 2 = moderate, 3 = severe

13

Creating a Treatment Contract

Why Contract?

As part of your management of your bipolar disorder, we recommend the use of a written care plan or treatment contract. The treatment contract gives you an opportunity to decide what you want to happen when you are ill. Designing this plan when you are well allows you to specify which management strategies are preferable to cope with severe episodes. This process involves selecting and educating a support system that will participate with you on your treatment contract. Recall from Chapter 1 that your support system may include your doctors, your family members, spouse or significant other, friends, coworkers, and so on. It is important that your support system receive information about bipolar disorder. They can read this book and, most importantly, listen to you about your specific symptoms. You may also invite your support system to attend one of your meetings with your psychiatrist or therapist.

To involve your support system, you must specify ways in which they can be helpful to you during acute episodes. You also may wish to give permission to your

> *The treatment contract gives you an opportunity to decide what you want to happen when you are ill.*

support system to contact your treatment team when they detect early symptoms of mania.

We would like you to empower your support system by instructing them to anticipate problems and informing them of the types of reactions and responses you would want them to make. By planning ahead when you are feeling relatively well, you maintain maximal control. Your support team will become agents of *your plan,* not people imposing restrictions on you.

By writing a treatment contract, you and your family members will have an action plan to use in case of future episodes. The treatment contract will enable you to take part in the planning and to exercise choice and control regarding what will happen throughout the course of your bipolar mood disorder and its treatment. Once the treatment contract is signed, your clinicians and family members or support system become agents of your plan, not people controlling your decisions. This approach will allow you to plan ahead during periods of calm in anticipation of the periods of stormy weather that may lie ahead.

Format of the Contract

Your individualized treatment contract begins with a review of the purpose of the contract and an identification of your support team. Then, you specify the characteristic thoughts, feelings, behaviors, and early warning signs for your episodes of depression. Keeping in mind that the symptoms of depression can vary from person to person, you want to personalize the treatment contract to reflect your experience of depression. Next, you specify a plan for coping with depression by stating ways in which your support system can be helpful to you.

Finally, you note the thoughts, feelings, and behaviors and early warning signs of hypomania and mania. You specify a plan for coping with mania or hypomania, giving specific instructions to the members of your support system. For example, instructions might include, "Call my doctor," or "Take away my credit cards." You may also want to specify who initiates the plan for mania. It is often your family or support system who will first recognize the signs of mania. You can also include other modules that target high-risk behaviors, such as substance abuse, bulimia, gambling, and so on, if these are problematic for you.

Your Contract

The contract on the following pages is both a guide for you to use in developing your personalized treatment contract and a kind of generic contract that you may want to fill out so you can have a plan in place while you work on a more personalized plan. Use it to reach the goal of getting your first treatment contract written. As you learn more about your condition and what works or doesn't work for you, the contract can be revised.

Use the following template as a guide. As you personalize the contract to reflect your individuality, feel free to cross out any text you feel is inappropriate or add items you think will be helpful. Your contract should reflect your preferences and should incorporate as much about what you know about yourself as possible.

The most important thing about having a plan is making sure you and everyone who agrees to participate in it actually follows the plan. As you gain experience with this approach to treatment, you will see that knowing who and what you can count on can be the glue that keeps everything together.

Treatment Contract

The purpose of this contract is to organize my care for bipolar disorder, with attention to both the prevention of mood episodes and the efficient treatment of these episodes should they occur. My first step in guiding my care is the selection of my support team. The team members should include people with whom I have regular contact, who can help me identify episodes should they occur and help me put into practice some of the tools discussed in previous chapters of this book.

(Select members of your treatment team to be part of your support team; for example, you may select your psychiatrist, psychologist, social worker, or primary care physician. Other team members may be drawn from the support network identified by you in Chapter 1.)

Treatment Contract: Support Team

Role/relationship	Name	Contact information
My psychiatrist	_____	Phone: _____
My therapist	_____	Phone: _____
My PCP	_____	Phone: _____
_____	_____	Phone: _____
_____	_____	Phone: _____
_____	_____	Phone: _____

My second step in developing this contract is to identify tools I will use to help control my bipolar disorder so that I can best pursue my life goals. Many of these tools have been identified in previous chapters. My goal now is to identify some of the tools that I want to plan to use.

For every tool or strategy listed, please place a checkmark next to the ones you plan to incorporate as a part of your treatment contract.

Monitor My Mood for Early Intervention

Signs of depression and mania are listed in Chapter 2. In addition to these symptoms, I know from my own patterns that I should watch out for the following signs.

Depressed thoughts _____

_____

_____

Depressed symptoms _____

_____

_____

Depressed behavior _____

_____

_____

Hypomanic thoughts _____

_____

_____

Hypomanic symptoms _____

_____

_____

Hypomanic behaviors_____

_____

_____

Take Early Action if I Notice Signs of Depression or Mania

Contact my psychiatrist at phone no._____.

Contact my therapist at phone no._____.

Contact my support person at phone no._____.

Maintain a regular schedule of sleep and activities.

Maintain a regular schedule of pleasant events.

Evaluate my thoughts for negative or hyperpositive thinking.

Talk with my family about ways to cope.

Limit my alcohol use and avoid all nonmedication drugs.

Other _____.

Other _____.

Other _____.

Other _____.

Take Active Steps to Keep My Mood in the Desired Range

Take all medications as prescribed by my doctor.

Maintain regular appointments with my psychiatrist at _____/month.

Maintain regular appointments with my therapist at _____/month.

Keep a regular sleep schedule.

Maintain a schedule including at least three valued activities each day as a buffer against stress.

Avoid excessive use of alcohol.

Avoid all use of illicit drugs.

Use no alcohol for the next 30 days.

Use no recreational drugs for the next 30 days.

Keep a perspective on my thoughts and evaluate my thoughts for accuracy.

Share with my family information on communication styles that may reduce stress.

Other _____.

Other _____.

Other _____.

Other _____.

Contact the Following People Should I Ever Have Strong Suicidal Thoughts

Contact my psychiatrist at phone no. _____.

Contact my therapist at phone no. _____.

Contact my support person at phone no. _____.

Other action _____.

Keep Myself Safe Until I Can Be Seen or Go to a Local Emergency Room if I Ever Fear I May Act on Suicidal Thoughts

If I Start to Become Depressed, I Would Like My Support Team to:

Talk to me about my symptoms (who _____)

Make plans for a pleasant event (who _____)

Discuss ways to reduce stress (who _____)

Make sure I am taking my medication (who _____)

Call my doctor if I am unable to (who _____)

Other _____

Other _____

Other _____

If I Start to Become Manic, I Would Like My Support Team to:

Talk to me about my symptoms (who _____)

Talk to me about reducing activities (who _____)

Allow me to be alone if I am irritable (who _____)

Take care of the kids/pets/other (who _____)

Take away my credit cards (who _____)

Take away my car keys (who _____)

Take me to the hospital (preferred hospital _____)

Other _____

Other _____

Other _____

I understand that this contract is designed by me so that I can take an active role in my treatment. My goal is to maximize my control by arranging for my support team to take care of me. So that any future decisions are well considered, I agree to change this contract only after giving two weeks written notice to all parties to this contract.

Signatures for Contracting Individuals

_____   _____

Signature   Date   Signature   Date

_____   _____

Signature   Date   Signature   Date

Improving Wellbeing

Our goals for this book were to provide you with a wide range of strategies for better managing bipolar disorder. Most of the strategies in this book were directed at reducing symptoms of mood disorders or reducing the stresses that can make mood episodes more likely. It would be a mistake, however, to focus on only the reduction of symptoms. It is also important to focus on the enhancement of positive emotions. In particular, we would like you to attend to those moments when you feel satisfied and pleasantly happy. We refer to these moments as periods of wellbeing.

With the term wellbeing we are referring to moments when you feel satisfied and happy. We are not referring to moments of particular excitement, achievement, or superiority, but of much quieter moments of wellbeing. This distinction is important, especially with respect to periods of hypomania. By focusing on wellbeing instead of hypomania, we are asking you to note and track periods of pleasantness (versus elation), satisfaction (versus excitement) and happiness (versus bliss). Most formally, we would like you to start a wellbeing diary, where, no matter what your dominant mood was, you are to select and write about the period of greatest wellbeing during each day.

Start a wellbeing diary so you can refer back to moments of pleasantness, satisfaction, and happiness in your life.

Buy a journal or notebook that appeals to you and represents who you are and use it as your wellbeing diary. Keep your diary in a handy place for daily entries. Most people will make their entries in the evening, but we would like you to make these entries long enough before bedtime that you have time to reflect back on what you wrote. The goal for the diary is to describe the feeling of wellbeing and the events (situations, interactions, or thoughts) that led to it. In addition to recording this information, we want to make sure that you become adept at *echoing* and increasing the frequency by which you experience wellbeing and the memory of wellbeing episodes. Echoing refers to the process of making sure that a pleasant event has reverberations during the day; that during periods where you might otherwise be daydreaming about problems, you take a moment to reflect on a period of wellbeing (from earlier that day or a previous day). In that way, the wellbeing period will echo across the day allowing you to relive these feelings. This echoing will naturally enhance your interest in planning additional activities of this sort. In fact, we encourage you to ask yourself the following questions when thinking back on a particular period of wellbeing.

- How did the period of wellbeing come about?
- What brought it to an end?
- What seems like a good idea for having (planning for) another moment like this?
- What seems like a good idea for making that moment of wellbeing last longer or be better echoed during the day?

As you become adept at echoing periods of wellbeing in the evening, we would like you to expand this skill for more general use during your days. When in the car, at stoplights, what do you think about? If you are like most people, you are reviewing problems or demands on your time, making sure that some of the worst moments of your day are repeated over and over again. In contrast, you could be devoting that stoplight time to reviewing and re-feeling the positive moments of your day, and using these positive moments as a guide to what you want in your day tomorrow. This sort of echoing is not a substitute for problem solving, but for most people, the time at the stoplight is not problem solving either, it is idle worry. At the stoplight, we would rather have you doing active planning, active echoing of periods of wellbeing, active problem solving, or active listening to the radio– anything better than idle worry. The wellbeing diary is your training time for being skilled at noticing, remembering, and echoing forward those moments of your day when life is working for you.

The wellbeing diary also serves as an excellent record of pleasant moments over time. This is why it is important to write in your wellbeing diary with regularity, so that you develop a log that can guide you to the pleasant moments in your life. After two weeks of regular entries, set aside some time to turn the pages slowly and revisit the wellbeing moments of your days over time.

The good news is that by attending to your periods of wellbeing, tracking them, and putting effort into expanding them, you will be likely to reduce the recurrence of depressed mood, as well as treat more subtle symptoms of depression that did not go away as the more severe mood episode lifted. And we especially like that these benefits come not from trying to reduce negative aspects of your life, but instead from attending to the positive aspects of your life. This is important mood therapy–it is directed at increasing positive mood rather than reducing bad moods, but it serves to treat both depression and worry. In this way, wellbeing interventions are like the watering-the-flowers-not-the-weeds approach from Chapter 9. Placing attention on what is working rather than what is not working is a nice way of creating change.

Start your wellbeing diary as soon as possible, regardless of whether you are in a positive or negative mood. Even when you are depressed, it is both possible and beneficial to track the moments in a day when you do have relative wellbeing. When down and when feeling better, we want you to be good at noticing the range of situations and events that may increase wellbeing (e.g., when alone, when with others, during an activity, spontaneously when you did not expect it, etc.) and use this information to enhance these feelings in your life.

Putting It All Together

In pursuing wellbeing, monitoring your mood and thoughts, using communication strategies, applying anger management, or using any of the other skills introduced in this book, you are working to be a powerful force in the co-management of bipolar disorder. Whether you are applying these skills for yourself or for a family member, the goal is to have you better meet your life goals while enhancing positive feelings. Our hope is that, over time, you will revisit this book and the Self-Guided Care boxes that ask you to actively rehearse component skills. Bipolar disorder requires you to be a specialist with many of these skills in order to have better control over moods. By working together with your treatment team and proactively working to manage stress and moods while enhancing the quality of your relationships, you have taken important steps to getting the quality of life that you deserve.

Index

Abilify, 23
active collaborators, 4
activities
    destructive, 73–74
    mania and, 93
    for mood stabilization, 63–67
    social skills and, 67
    valued, 61–62
activity charting, 74*t*
    work and, 60–61
ADD. *See* attention deficit
    disorder
ADHD. *See* attention-deficit-
    hyperactivity disorder
adolescent(s)
    alcohol and, 48, 52–53
    bipolar disorder and, 12
    education and, 42
after-school programs, 49
aggression, 94
agitation, 21, 94
alcohol, 73
    adolescents and, 48, 52–53
    bipolar disorder and, 74
alcoholism, 14
all-or-nothing thinking, 76
alprazolam, 25
angel dust, 73

anger, 93
    arguments and, 93, 97–98
    conflicts and, 97–98
    coping skills, 94–95
    depression and, 93
    goals and, 98–99
    hypomania and, 93–94
    management, 94
    mania and, 93
    poor thinking habits
      and, 95–96
    reducing, 94
    relationships and, 94
    remembering goals
      and, 98–99
    thinking patterns and, 95–96
    victimization and, 96
    win/lose thinking, 97–98
antianxiety medications. *See*
    anxiolytics
antidepressants, 14
    anxiety and, 18
    common, 24*t*
    communication and, 20
    depression and, 20
    dosages of, 22*t*
    mania and, 20
    physicians and, 20–21

antipsychotics, 18, 22–23. *See also*
    atypical antipsychotic
        medications
    childhood bipolar
        disorder and, 44
    common, 26*t*
    dosages, 26*t*
    mania and, 21
anxiety
    antidepressants and, 18
    CBT and, 44
    childhood bipolar
        disorder and, 41
    disorders, 14
    exercise and, 62
    mood charting and, 113*f*
    rating, 110
anxiolytics, 23–25
    insomnia and, 18
arguments. *See also* conflicts
    avoiding, 98–99
    finishing, 98
    irritability and anger
        and, 93, 97–98
aripiprazole, 19, 23
asenapine, 23
Ativan, 24
attention deficit disorder
    (ADD), 14
attention-deficit-hyperactivity
    disorder (ADHD), 41
    college planning and, 46–47
atypical antipsychotic
    medications, 23
    children and, 43–44
Atypical Bipolar disorder. *See*
    Bipolar NOS

behavior. *See also* cognitive-behavior
    therapy
    changes in, 91
    high-risk, 117
benzodiazepines, 25
bipolar disorder(s), 5. *See also*
    childhood bipolar disorder(s)

adolescents and, 12
alcohol and, 74
causes of, 13
college and, 50, 53
commonality of, 12
controlling, 18
coping with, 15
course of, 12–13
emerging of, 50
episodes, 57
family and, 14, 85–86
hopelessness and, 81
medications for, 17–18
postpartum, 13
protective factors, 14*t*
psychotherapy and, 33–34
remission of, 13
risk factors, 14*t*
stimulants and, 73
stress and, 13, 57
substance abuse and, 13, 73–74
subtypes of, 9–11
suicidal thoughts, 81–82
summary of, 10*t*
women and, 12, 31
Bipolar I, 9–10
Bipolar II, 10–11
Bipolar NOS (Not Otherwise
    Specific), 11
Black Thinking, 76
bulimia, 14, 117

Calan, 19
carbamazepine, 19
CBT. *See* cognitive-behavior
    therapy
cell phone, 49
children
    anxiety and, 41
    atypical antipsychotic
        medications and, 43–44
    bipolar disorder in, 12, 39
    comorbidity and, 41
    course of illness in, 41
    depression in, 39

education and, 45–46
emotional instability and, 42
mania and, 39–40
mixed episodes in, 40
mood stabilizers and, 43
school supports and, 45–46
suicidal thoughts in, 40
childbirth, 13
childhood bipolar disorder(s), 39
antipsychotics and, 44
anxiety and, 41
attitude and, 51
CBT and, 44
college and, 42, 46–47
course of, 41
evaluation of, 43
impact of, 41–42
medications and, 43–44
parenting strategies for, 47–48
psychotherapy and, 44–45
school and, 42
stimulants and, 44
substance abuse and, 44, 48
treatment of, 43
chlorpromazine, 22
clinicians. *See also* physicians
communication with, 91–92
mood charting and, 111
clonazepam, 24
clozapine, 23
cocaine, 73
cognitive-behavior
therapy (CBT), 35
anxiety and, 44
childhood bipolar
disorder and, 44
communication and, 35
coping skills and, 44
social skills and, 44
thinking patterns and, 44
college
ADHD and, 46–47
bipolar disorder and, 50, 53
childhood bipolar disorder
and, 42

planning around, 46–47
transitioning and, 50
communication
antidepressants and, 20
CBT and, 35
with clinicians, 91–92
conditions for, 88
effective listening, 88–89
family and, 87–90
FFT and, 35
improving, 86
IPT and, 35
self-care, 87–90
skills, 87–90
solutions and, 87
strategies, 85
techniques, 86
comorbidity
children and, 41
DSM-IV-TR and, 14
conduct disorder. *See*
oppositional-defiant
disorder
conflicts. *See also* arguments
family and, 85–86
irritability and anger
and, 97–98
consequences, negative, 79
coping skills
CBT and, 44
irritability and anger
and, 94–95
side effects and, 30
counseling, in-school, 46
couples' therapy, 89–90
crisis plans, 49
criticism, 77
requesting changes in behavior
and, 91
cyclothymia, 11

dancing, 66
daydreaming, 126
delusions, 21
Depakote, 19, 43

depression. *See also* antidepressants
Bipolar I, 9–10
Bipolar II, 10–11
Bipolar NOS and, 11
in children, 39
consistent use of medications
and, 25
definition of, 8–9
DSM-IV-TR and, 6
early action on, 120
episodes of, 85, 93
exercise and, 62
hypomania and, 8
irritability and anger and, 93
life goals and, 101
manic, 5
motivations for medication use
and, 30
sleep and, 24, 58–59
suicidal thoughts and, 81–82
symptoms of, 9
symptom summary, 7*t*
thinking patterns and, 76–77
treatment contracts and, 116
wellbeing and, 127
destructive activities, 73–74
diagnosis of psychiatric problems, 6
Diagnostic and Statistical Manual,
4th edition, text revision.
See DSM-IV-TR
diazepam, 25
dopamine, 21–23
dosages, 17, 25
of antidepressants, 22*t*
of antipsychotics, 26*t*
of mood stabilizers, 24*t*
DSM-IV-TR (*Diagnosis and
Statistical Manual,* 4th
edition, text revision), 6
comorbidity and, 14
episodes, 7*t*

echoing, 126
education. *See also* college
adolescents and, 42
children and, 45–46
planning, 46–47
effective listening, 88
strategies, 89
emergency services, 83
emotions
instability in children, 42
positive, 125
Eskalith, 19
evaluation, 68
exercise, 62–63
anxiety and, 62
depression and, 62
for mood stabilizing, 62–63
stress and, 62

family
bipolar disorder and, 14, 85–86
communication skills
and, 87–90
conflicts, 85–86
medications and, 28
therapy, 44
family-focused therapy (FFT), 35
FDA (Food and Drug
Administration), 20, 23
feedback
negative, 87
positive, 88
verbal, 88
FFT. *See* family-focused therapy
frustration, 94

gambling, 117
genetics, 13. *See also* family
Geodon, 23
goals. *See also* life goals
irritability and anger and, 98–99
long-term, 35
pacing, 105–6
self-care and, 105–6
starting point of, 105
taking medication and, 28

grandiosity, 40
guilt, 98

Haldol, 22
hallucinations, 21
haloperidol, 22
happiness, 125–26
headaches, migraine, 14
hobbies, 61
homework, 45
hopelessness, 81
hospitals, 49
hyperpositive
    thinking, 78–79, 120
hypomania, 78
    Bipolar II and, 10–11
    Bipolar NOS and, 11
    children and, 39
    coping with, 116
    definition of, 8
    DSM-IV-TR and, 6
    irritability and anger
        and, 93–94
    sleep problems and, 24
    symptoms of, 8
    symptom summary, 7*t*
    wellbeing and, 125

IEP. *See* Individualized Education
    Plan
IM. *See* instant messenger
individuality, 117
Individualized Education Plan
    (IEP), 45
insomnia, 18
instant messenger (IM), 49
internet, 49
interpersonal psychotherapy
    (IPT), 35
interventions
    early, 119
    wellbeing, 127
IPT. *See* interpersonal
    psychotherapy

irritability
    arguments and, 93, 97–98
    conflicts and, 97–98
    coping skills for, 94–95
    depression and, 93
    hypomania and, 93–94
    mania and, 93
    mood charting and, 113*f*
    rating, 110
    reducing, 94
    relationships and, 94
    remembering goals
        and, 98–99
    win/lose thinking, 97–98
Isoptin, 19

job functioning, 101
journals, 126–27

ketamine (special K), 73
Klonopin, 25

Lamictal, 19
lamotrigine, 19
language therapy, 46
learning disabilities, 45–46
leisure, 60–61
life disruptions, 101–2
life events
    course of, 101
    positive, 73
life goals, 101
    clarifying of, 104
    depression and, 101
    markers of, 102–3
    pacing of, 105–6
    paths to, 102*f*
    starting, 105
    strategies, 102–3
listening, effective, 88–89
lithium, 19, 43
Lithobid, 19
loaded words, 75, 78
lorazepam, 24

mania, 78. *See also* hypomania
  activities and, 93
  antidepressants and, 20
  antipsychotics and, 21
  Bipolar I, 9–10
  children and, 39–40
  consistent use of medication
    and, 29
  coping with, 116–17
  definition of, 6
  DSM-IV-TR and, 6
  early action on, 120
  episodes of, 85
  irritability and anger and, 93
  life disruptions and, 101
  motivations for medication use
    and, 30
  olanzapine, 19
  sleep and, 24, 58–59
  symptoms of, 6, 7t
  treatment contracts and, 122
manic depression, 5
marveling, 76, 83
medications. *See also specific*
    medications or medication
    types
  bipolar disorder and, 17–18
  childhood bipolar disorder
    and, 43–44
  classification of, 18
  consistent use of, 28–29
  control and, 51
  depression and, 25
  dosages of, 17
  family and, 28
  issues with, 51
  mania and, 29–30
  monitoring, 31
  mood episodes and, 51
  motivations for, 30
  necessity of, 17
  pregnancy and, 31–32
  relapses and, 19
  self-care and, 30
  symptoms and, 29

  taking, 27–28
  types of, 18
Mellaril, 22
men, 12
menstruation, 111
migraine headaches, 14
misunderstandings, 88
mixed episodes
  in children, 40
  DSM-IV-TR and, 6
  symptom summary, 7t
mood(s)
  depression *v.*, 8–9
  desired range of, 120–21
  disorders, 5
  disturbance, 94
  episodes, 5, 39, 51, 57,
    83, 85, 111
  exercise and, 62–63
  keeping schedules
    and, 60
  mania and, 6, 78
  monitoring, 31
  patterns in, 111
  stabilizing activities, 63–67
  symptoms, 5–6
mood charting, 92, 112f
  anxiety and, 113f
  clinicians and, 111
  completing, 110–10
  importance of, 109–10
  irritability and anger and, 113f
  routines and, 110
  sleep and, 113f
  treatment team and, 109
mood stabilizers, 18–20
  children and, 43
  common, 24t
  dosages of, 24t
muscle relaxation
    techniques, 58

napping, 59
Navane, 22
negative feedback, 87

neuroleptics, 22. *See also* antipsychotics
neurotransmitters, 21

obsessive-compulsive disorder (OCD), 14
occupational therapy, 46
OCD. *See* obsessive-compulsive disorder
ODD. *See* oppositional-defiant disorder
olanzapine, 19
Omega-3 fatty acids, 19
oppositional-defiant disorder (ODD), 41
options, 68
overconfidence, 78–79
oxcarbazepine, 19

pacing, of goals, 105–6
parenting strategies, 47–48
Paxil, 21
PCP, 73
perphenazine, 22
personal attacks, 96
personalization, 76
perspective, 89
pets, 42, 122
phone numbers, 82–83
physicians
    antidepressants and, 20–21
    side effects and, 29
pleasantness, 125
positive emotions, 125
positive feedback, 88
positive life events, 73
pregnancy. *See* childbirth
problem solving
    process, 68
    scheduling time for, 67–68
    self-care, 68–72
    strategies, 68
protective factors, 14*t*
psychotherapy, 33. *See also specific psychotherapy modalities*

childhood bipolar disorder and, 44–45
    specific, 34–36
psychotic episodes, 73
punishment, 91

quetiapine, 19, 23

rapid cycling, 12, 39
recreation, 62
regret, 98
relapses, 19
relationships
    communication skills and, 85–86
    irritability and anger and, 94
risk
    factors, 14*t*
    underestimating, 78
Risperdal, 44
risperidone, 23
routines, 31
    mood charting and, 110

safety strategies, 82–83
Saphris, 23
satisfaction, 125
schedules. *See also* routines
    keeping, 60
    management of, 57–59
    problem solving, 67–68
    regular, 60
    time, 61–62
schizophrenia, 21
school counseling, 46
school supports, 45–46
Section 504 plan, 45
self-care
    achieving goals, 105–6
    communication, 87–90
    medications and, 30
    for mood stabilization, 63–67
    problem solving, 68–72
    sleep and, 58

self-care (*Cont'd*)
    suicidal thoughts and, 81–82
    thinking patterns and, 80–81
    valued activities, 61–62
self-talk, 83, 96
Seroquel, 23, 44
serotonin, 23
shame, 91
should statements, 102–3
    pacing of goals and, 105–6
side effects, 31
    coping skills and, 30
    physicians and, 29
    treatment teams and, 31
sleep
    depression and, 24, 58–59
    hypomania and, 24
    insomnia, 18
    mania and, 24, 58–59
    mood charting and, 113*f*
    patterns, 57–59
    problems, 24–25
    self-care and, 58
    stress and, 57
    techniques, 58–59
    traveling and, 59
    treatment contracts and, 120
social skills
    activities, 67
    CBT and, 44
solutions, 87
sounds, 93
special K. *See* ketamine
speech therapy, 46
speed, 73
stability, 101
stimulants, 14
    bipolar disorder and, 73
    childhood bipolar disorder
      and, 44
strategies
    communication, 85
    coping with irritability and
      anger, 94
    effective listening, 89

life goals, 102–3
parenting, 47–48
problem solving, 68
safety, 82–83
stress
    bipolar disorder and, 13, 57
    exercise and, 62
    minimization of, 85
    positive events and, 73
    schedule management and,
      57–59
    sleep and, 57
substance abuse, 14, 25, 52–53,
    117. *See also specific substances*
    avoiding, 73–74
    bipolar disorder and, 13, 73–74
    childhood bipolar disorder
      and, 44, 48
    treatment contracts and, 117
suicidal thoughts
    bipolar disorder and, 81–82
    in children, 40
    depression and, 81–82
    self-care and, 81–82
    symptoms and, 81
    treatment contracts and, 121–22
    warning signs, 81–82
suicide prevention plan, 83
support groups, 49
support team(s). *See also* treatment
    team(s)
    instructions for, 116–17
    treatment contracts and, 118
symptoms
    of depression, 9
    of hypomania, 8
    of mania, 6
    mood episodes and, 5–6
    suicidal thoughts and, 81
    taking medication and, 29

tardive dyskinesia (TD), 23
TD. *See* tardive dyskinesia
Tegretol, 19
textbooks, 46

therapists, 33–34
 selecting, 36–38
therapy. *See also* psychotherapy
 CBT, 35, 44
 couples', 89–90
 family and, 44
 FFT, 35
 IPT, 35
 language, 46
 occupational, 46
 speech, 46
thinking biases, 75–78
thinking patterns. *See also*
  suicidal thoughts
 accurate perspective on, 79, 83
 all-or-nothing, 76
 anger and, 95–96
 Black, 76
 CBT and, 44
 coaching, 75, 77, 96
 depression and, 76–77
 emotions and, 75–76
 hyperpositive, 78–79, 120
 inaccurate, 79
 managing, 35
 negative, 75–76
 poor habits, 95–96
 self-care and, 80–81
 treatment contracts and, 120
 White, 76
 win/lose, 97–98
thioridazine, 22
thioxixene, 22
Thorazine, 22
time scheduling, 61–62
traveling, 59
treatment contracts, 115
 depression and, 116
 example of, 118–23
 format of, 116–17
 high-risk behaviors and, 117
 mania and, 122
 personalization of, 117
 purpose of, 117–18
 sleep and, 120

substance abuse and, 117
 suicidal thoughts and, 121–22
 support team, 118
 thinking patterns and, 120
treatment team(s)
 mood charting and, 109
 side effects and, 31
 therapists and, 33–34
Trilafon, 22
Trileptal, 19

unipolar disorders, 9, 10*t*

Valium, 25
valproate, 19
verapamil, 19
verbal feedback, 88
victimization, 96
volunteering, 65

watering the flowers, 87
weight, 111
wellbeing, 128
 echoing, 126
 hypomania and, 125
 interventions, 127
 journals and, 126–27
Wellbutrin-SR, 21
whisper rule, 86
White Thinking, 76
Why Game, 103–4
win/lose thinking, 97–98
within normal limits (WNL), 110
WNL. *See* within normal limits
women, 12, 31
work, activity charting
  and, 60–61
worry, 58
written care plan. *See* treatment
  contracts

Xanax, 25

ziprasidone, 19, 23
Zyprexa, 19, 23, 44